Using Other People's Money to Get Rich:

Secrets, Techniques, and Strategies Investors Use Every Day Using OPM to Make Millions

By Desiree Smith-Daughety

USING OTHER PEOPLE'S MONEY TO GET RICH: SECRETS, TECHNIQUES, AND STRATEGIES INVESTORS USE EVERY DAY USING OPM TO MAKE MILLIONS

Copyright © 2010 Atlantic Publishing Group, Inc.
1405 SW 6th Avenue • Ocala, Florida 34471 • Phone 800-814-1132 • Fax 352-622-1875
Web site: www.atlantic-pub.com • E-mail: sales@atlantic-pub.com
SAN Number: 268-1250

Library of Congress Cataloging-in-Publication Data

Smith-Daughety, Desiree, 1968-
  Using other people's money to get rich : secrets, techniques, and strategies investors use every day using OPM to make millions / by Desiree Smith-Daughety.
    p. cm.
  Includes bibliographical references and index.
  ISBN-13: 978-1-60138-214-6 (alk. paper)
  ISBN-10: 1-60138-214-6 (alk. paper)
  1. New business enterprises--Finance. 2. Venture capital. 3. Entrepreneurship. I. Title.
  HG4027.6.S65 2009
  658.15'2--dc22
                          2009042368

Printed in the United States

PROJECT MANAGER: Erin Everhart • eeverhart@atlantic-pub.com
PEER REVIEWER: Marilee Griffin • mgriffin@atlantic-pub.com
ASSISTANT EDITOR: Angela Pham • apham@atlantic-pub.com
INTERIOR DESIGN: James Ryan Hamilton • www.jamesryanhamilton.com
FRONT & BACK COVER DESIGN: Jackie Miller • millerjackiej@gmail.com

Printed on Recycled Paper

We recently lost our beloved pet "Bear," who was not only our best and dearest friend but also the "Vice President of Sunshine" here at Atlantic Publishing. He did not receive a salary but worked tirelessly 24 hours a day to please his parents. Bear was a rescue dog that turned around and showered myself, my wife, Sherri, his grandparents Jean, Bob, and Nancy, and every person and animal he met (maybe not rabbits) with friendship and love. He made a lot of people smile every day.

We wanted you to know that a portion of the profits of this book will be donated to The Humane Society of the United States. –*Douglas & Sherri Brown*

The human-animal bond is as old as human history. We cherish our animal companions for their unconditional affection and acceptance. We feel a thrill when we glimpse wild creatures in their natural habitat or in our own backyard.

Unfortunately, the human-animal bond has at times been weakened. Humans have exploited some animal species to the point of extinction.

The Humane Society of the United States makes a difference in the lives of animals here at home and worldwide. The HSUS is dedicated to creating a world where our relationship with animals is guided by compassion. We seek a truly humane society in which animals are respected for their intrinsic value, and where the human-animal bond is strong.

Want to help animals? We have plenty of suggestions. Adopt a pet from a local shelter, join The Humane Society and be a part of our work to help companion animals and wildlife. You will be funding our educational, legislative, investigative and outreach projects in the U.S. and across the globe.

Or perhaps you'd like to make a memorial donation in honor of a pet, friend or relative? You can through our Kindred Spirits program. And if you'd like to contribute in a more structured way, our Planned Giving Office has suggestions about estate planning, annuities, and even gifts of stock that avoid capital gains taxes.

Maybe you have land that you would like to preserve as a lasting habitat for wildlife. Our Wildlife Land Trust can help you. Perhaps the land you want to share is a backyard—that's enough. Our Urban Wildlife Sanctuary Program will show you how to create a habitat for your wild neighbors.

So you see, it's easy to help animals. And The HSUS is here to help.

2100 L Street NW • Washington, DC 20037 • 202-452-1100
www.hsus.org

Acknowledgements

I am grateful for the support of my family. This is dedicated to Cameron and to the future wave of entrepreneurs — may we all get caught dreaming more often.

Trademark Disclaimer

All trademarks, trade names, or logos mentioned or used are the property of their respective owners and are used only to directly describe the products being provided. Every effort has been made to properly capitalize, punctuate, identify, and attribute trademarks and trade names to their respective owners, including the use of ® and ™ wherever possible and practical. Atlantic Publishing Group, Inc. is not a partner, affiliate, or licensee with the holders of said trademarks.

Table of Contents

Chapter 10: Managing OPM 201

Chapter 11: Real Estate Investment with OPM 229

Chapter 12: Other Uses of OPM 255

Foreword

Using Other People's Money to Get Rich

I f you are a true entrepreneur, just reading the title *Using Other People's Money to Get Rich* should get your juices flowing, your engine revving, and make your mouth water like there are steaks on the grill and cold beer in the fridge. I could go on all day about a title that good — so good I wish I had written it myself.

If you are new to the game of investing, let me break it down for you: Using other people's money is the only way to get rich — the only right way, that is. Sure, you can bootstrap; you can roll pennies; you can save, scrimp, watch, go without, and suffer all the livelong day — but that does not make it right or efficient. In business, there is nothing noble about suffering if you do not have enough money.

I have counseled, worked with, and been a bootstrapping entrepreneur since I was 8 years old — I learned at the foot of the master, my dad — and I can tell you I was struggling to start a business, going without a salary, barely (or not) making ends meet, and wondering when something is going to break through the dark clouds, when someone finally pointed it out to me: You are doing it all wrong.

I had reached a point in my business when I simply could not go it alone anymore. I could not expand without fresh, outside capital — my cash flow would not be enough. I needed other people's money.

I rewrote my business plan to reflect the fact that I needed a cash injection to bring my business back to life and get me where I was headed. I gave it to a friend of mine who was an investment banker to critique. His response changed my life. He said, "It's a great business plan, but you're not asking for enough money."

After the initial stun wore off, my first thought was: Where have you been all my life?

He was right, of course. I was new to asking strangers for large sums of money. I had been getting by with businesses my entire life, and I did not think I would ever need to raise outside capital, but I was wrong, and my wrong attitude was reflected in the business plan cash flow statement.

First of all, my No. 1 mistake was that I did not take a salary for myself. Do not ever deny yourself a salary. You are not being noble or showing some good faith with this gesture unless you are already financially free, which is when your passive income beats your bills each month without needing to draw a salary from the new business. However, if the most you have ever made in your life is $120,000, and suddenly this "job" gives you a $300,000 salary, you will not make it past the first potential investor. But smart and ethical investors do not want to see you hurting for a living while you are turning their risk capital into more capital for them. They want you focused on the business at hand,

and not focused on how to make rent or the car payment, whilst you burn through their cash for your business.

My second mistake: I did not ask for enough money (initially) for working capital. I whittled down the projected expenses and cost of goods sold (COGS) to almost nothing, thinking that if we cut here and there and do not use a napkin for every lunch, we might make it work. I painted an unrealistic scenario in potential investors' minds, namely that everything is going to go right, immediately.

Thirdly, I showed cash flow too soon. While I knew we could be cash-flow positive in three months, my investment banker friend said, "Make it six — just in case." Again, thanks to his advice, I wrote the plan that got funded, not the plan of my best-case scenario in business.

But my biggest mistake, one I made out of ignorance and vow never to make again, was that I did not start my business with other people's money.

I believe that every successful and easy — relatively speaking, we are talking about making something from nothing, here — business owner uses OPM to his or her greatest advantage. You are not a business until you are paying the bills — including your salary and something near the projected return to your investors — with your own internally generated cash flow. Until that moment, all you have is an idea you have talked some friends into and maybe secured some financing for.

As good as the title of this book, it is the content inside the covers that sets it apart. *Using Other People's Money to Get Rich: Secrets,*

Techniques, and Strategies Investors Use Every Day Using OPM to Make Millions is excellent from start to finish. I daresay it is the complete and only guide you will ever need — at least until a new form of OPM is invented — to get rich in business. I mean that literally. Every which way to get funded in business is in this book. I read it. I loved it. I wish I had it years ago.

I will give you one piece of advice that is very hard for an entrepreneur to hear, let alone do: Whatever you read in this book, just do it. Just do it like she wrote it and you will get your money, and you will have your business, and you will be happy you did. And you can thank her (and me) later.

Foreword Author Biography

Anthony Migyanka is the host of Mutual Fund Circus™ television show on Biz Television and the executive producer of Mutual Fund Circus for Kids™, a program for children's financial literacy. Migyanka has appeared on "Cavuto" with Neil Cavuto, and is recognized by the Fox Business News as an investor relations expert. He has also contributed public company governance, as well as stock market and economic trend commentary, to other media outlets, including FamilyNet TV, the Dow Jones Corporation, and the *Washington Post*. Migyanka created "The Golden Ticket Mortgage Plan" for homeowner relief, submitted to the Homeowner Preservation Office of the U.S. Treasury and Federal Reserve. Migyanka also writes the monthly personal finance column for the *SHI Symbol International* e-magazine. He has recently been named a business insight expert by **yourBusinessChannel.com**.

Preface

"Knowledge is power."
Sir Francis Bacon, *Religious Meditations, Of Heresies,* 1597,
English author and philosopher

Although no calendar includes a date with this name on it, many people seem to cling desperately to "someday" as if it will miraculously appear on the horizon, making all of their wishes instantly come true. Your dreams do not need to wait for "someday."

If you want to live your dreams, start thinking in terms of today. By purchasing this book, you have already made the most important first step to realizing your dreams: gaining the necessary knowledge to make it happen.

Opportunities abound; there is an incredible number of opportunities that will help you achieve your dreams. You just need to learn what they are, decide which ones will work for you, and how to take advantage of them.

What you need is a willingness to set aside the notion of "someday" and adopt an action-oriented mindset that relies on what can be done today. Today is a day that you can transform into that "someday," as it is as good as any other day.

Your dreams are waiting to be fulfilled, so let us get started.

Introduction

Why Use Other People's Money?

Using other people's money (OPM, as you will see it referred to throughout the book) is becoming a common practice because it is a highly effective method for building wealth. With OPM, you can launch a business venture, grow an existing business, or acquire property.

For years, the way people went about earning wealth was limited to less than a handful of avenues:

1. They were born into a wealthy family.

2. They scrimped, saved, and went without in order to slowly coax a nest egg into hatching condition — if and when the time ever came.

3. They invented a product or service that customers clamored for.

The first one is purely a case of luck, and something you have no control over. The second is a case of gritting one's teeth in the hopes of creating something big. The last one is a combination of smarts, creativity, and luck.

But that last option was the only means that would bring you closer to wealth if you were not a person born into affluence — more than the option of scrimping and saving — hoping it would one day magically transform from nest egg to golden egg. The trouble is that although business ideas are thought up every day, many never go beyond the imagination of the person who dreams them up. Business ideas take money in order to move them from idea to reality.

Over time, people had to work on using the idea behind that third option — combining smarts with luck and a generous helping of creative thinking — refining the principles of it and coming up with another option that would be more likely to succeed.

Where better to look for inspiration than the already-wealthy? While they were at it, why not have these wealthy people take a look at one of their ideas and see if they found it intriguing enough to invest in? The pioneers of OPM were discovering the power of tapping into someone else's wealth for their own benefit, and in the long run, their investors could benefit, as well.

Build Wealth Now

Those OPM pioneers were hungry for wealth and were not willing to wait for money until after they had tightened their belts to the point they could no longer breathe. So, they found a way to get their ideas turned into deals and started rolling with them immediately, giving them the means to begin building true fortunes. It is a tradition of wealth-building that continues to this day.

There is no real science behind the use of OPM to build wealth. Rather, what you will find is that it involves a good dose of common sense. OPM is built on the principles of doing good business and has as its foundation the ideals of the American dream, which is based on the pursuit of one's goals in life that define happiness in one's eyes.

Many people are under the impression that they have to have money in order to get money. Well, it is true, but not in the way you may think. Just like the 17th century author John Ray said, "Money begets money." People usually take this saying too literally, believing it specifically means having their own money. Nothing could be further from the truth — or keep you more at arm's length from opportunities.

Do not be put off by the economic downturn that began in late 2008. Many seasoned investors look at a downturn as a gold mine rich in opportunities for those who dare. A downturn may be where you begin to build your empire. It may surprise — and inspire — you to know that many great companies got their start during challenging economic times, including IBM, HP, Hershey's, Texas Instruments, and Microsoft. Challenging markets can spawn incredible innovation and creativity.

By using OPM, you can launch your business idea to service a sector of the market that has a need for which you have a product, or you can begin investing in real estate to fulfill your dream of renovating homes. In return, the person whose money you are using will also benefit. Maybe they will earn money from their investment in your enterprise. Or maybe they will own a stake in your business. With risk comes the potential of great reward, and that is what OPM is all about — for both the dreamer and investor.

Using Other People's Money to Get Rich is going to show you the techniques that people are using to create wealth and reach their goals today, and not some hazy, undefined day that will hopefully happen in the future. By taking your ideas, dreams, and goals, and applying to them the techniques and advice outlined here — you too can gain the type of wealth that would have otherwise taken you an untold number of years to attain. You want to enjoy the benefits of having wealth now — not when you are too old to enjoy it or care — ending up having created a nice inheritance for everyone else down your family line. Why wait another 10, 20, or 30 years to be able to invest in the ventures that will create wealth and comfort now?

You are not the only one who benefits from the opportunity of using other people's money: Those people benefit, as well. Otherwise, OPM would not have survived as a concept or common practice. It is a win-win situation, and in these pages you will learn why. You will also meet others in these pages through case studies, getting a glimpse as to how they once stood exactly where you are now, forged ahead, and made the leap into prosperity.

Dream Big – Your Goals Depend On It

You have the capability to start creating a fortune that may otherwise be impossible without the use of someone else's money in order to make that opportunity happen.

So while you are imagining the possibilities — dream big.

Using the principle of other people's money, an entire empire can be built within a matter of months. An example of the critical importance and relevance of dreaming big is illustrated by the company Archadeck, an outdoor construction franchise that specializes in decks, patios, awnings, and other wood garden structures. To run this business and build these types of projects, a substantial amount of money is needed up-front to negotiate the building materials, fees, and carpenter pay. The Archadeck method uses the tactic of negotiating for partial payments throughout the stages of the building process. The problem with this is, even with a more balanced cash flow, the business will not always be able to secure enough money to cover basic running costs and marketing, which can make or break such a business.

The only way to start a business is to have the necessary capital up-front to carry the business at least six months, with or without customers. This will ensure a smooth-running operation even through the normal cyclical ups and downs of the building season. To further show how this works, here is a breakdown of it in action using the story of two dedicated Archadeck franchise owners, both of whom had the same potential — but only one managed to build a profitable business, while the other had to close his shop after three years, saddled with a large debt.

The first franchise owner went into business with the conservative idea of getting his feet wet and slowly building the business to the point where it would be able to stand on its own. The second franchise owner went into partnership with a silent partner who agreed to front a large sum of money to cover the cost of a year of aggressive advertising, general operating costs, and taxes.

To make a long and unfortunate story short, the conservative franchise owner had handicapped his potential from the beginning by not advertising effectively, had cash flow issues during the building process (creating unhappy customers and poor references), and was unable to pay carpenters, office staff, and taxes. His business was doomed because he did not utilize OPM to ensure a healthy beginning and, therefore, a greater chance of business success. The other franchise owner who used OPM started out with the same difficulties as any other new business owner would but was able to use the available money to overcome the inevitable bumps along the road. He eventually created a smoothly running business that could support itself within a year.

The moral of the story is that it is better to give your business venture full potential by allowing it a generous amount of funds from its very inception. In the end, you will spend this money anyway, so it works to your advantage to do it initially rather than slowly bleeding your business to death by trying to save money that is too vital to do without, or working overtime doing damage control after the fact. This is one of many stories of how OPM can be beneficial to creating wealth and stability in an easier and shorter duration than your average, middle-class citizens are able to do on their own.

CASE STUDY: THE BANDY GROUP

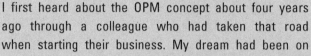

www.sarahbandy.com

Sarah Bandy – Real Estate Agent, Entrepreneur, and President of the Bandy Group

I first heard about the OPM concept about four years ago through a colleague who had taken that road when starting their business. My dream had been on hold for about two years before I began my quest to use OPM. I found my OPM through networking events. When I began the process to secure OPM, my greatest fear was not succeeding or reaching my goal; I did not want to disappoint the one person who believed in me. But once the OPM contributor told me not to make any promises and to just do my best, I was able to relax and truly set out to achieve my goals.

If you are sitting on the fence, not sure if you should use OPM, my best advice would be to just go for it. OPM is a numbers game: Most will say no, but someone will say yes. And keep in mind that we do not always end up where we start at the outset of our journey. I had been successful in the past, but a few curve balls left me in a different position in life. OPM helped me to get my confidence back. It allowed me to realize that my vision and passion could be seen and felt by someone else, and it made me stronger in order to continue and reach the next level.

Entrepreneurs should view OPM as the first step on their 1,000-mile journey. They should embrace that resource and realize that when things take off and happen for them, it will happen for the OPM investor as well, ultimately making a great symbiotic relationship.

For my investor, offering funds to an entrepreneur meant giving someone a second chance at life. It meant trusting a person with no expectation other than to believe in them and their dream, and hope that the passion and drive — coupled with an interesting concept — would all yield greater rewards in the end.

To ensure that your investors are satisfied with the relationship, I recommend that entrepreneurs keep an open line of communication so that there are no misunderstandings. And when working with a new investor, you need to be prepared to present a time line with information as to who will effectuate said duties.

When I went to my OPM source to sell them on my idea, I think it made a difference that I went in and was myself. I did not pretend to be something I was not. I showed them my strong suits and was honest about my shortcomings.

Chapter 1:

The Basics of OPM

O nly your imagination limits the opportunities that can be created by using other people's money. However, understand that you need good ideas and solid planning in order for those ideas to be successfully launched. In order to get to that stage, though, you need to begin with your dreams. It will not cost you anything to dream as big as possible from the very beginning. You can always scale back later. It is better to allow your ideas to roam the full spectrum than trying to rein them in immediately. No need to worry just yet if your dreams are realistic. Both you and your ideas will be faced with practical reality soon enough. Before you get to that point, however, you want to make sure your planning efforts encompass the absolute best-case scenario and that you have prepared for the potential of huge success.

The main types of wealth-building opportunities fall under:

1. Business ownership

2. Real estate

3. Inventions

Within these headings, you have a broad spectrum of subtypes that will define your particular business. And once you have your business up, running, and profitable, then you will have the opportunity to then further grow your wealth. Paying off debt, making funds available for your children's education, or investing in another business — these are just some of the ways you can take advantage of the boost you get by using other people's money.

Without using someone else's financial resources to gain an advantage in creating your own resources, your dreams could very well remain where they are now: as floundering, vague concepts that never get launched. Your dreams will stay stuck in neutral if they have not been given the time, attention, and resources in order to bring them to fruition.

Wealth and success do not happen by accident (beyond the circumstances of the family you were born into, as mentioned in the Introduction). It takes research and strategic planning built on a solid idea. Once you decide to take the big step into the role of entrepreneur and carry through with your great business idea, there are two main directions in which you can go in order to get that business idea moved from the conceptual realm and into reality:

- The first choice depends on your already having personal assets at your disposal to be used to fund your venture. These personal assets can be in the form of real estate or a business that you currently own, stocks and bonds, and other investments. Using these assets would be considered an attempt to self-fund your project. This is not only risky for people who are using their life savings, but it can also take longer to accomplish the end goal, as well as be limited by the amount of available funds.

- The second choice is referred to as a taking strategic advantage by using other people's money to build your own wealth. By using OPM, you use the funds from one or more sources that have the capability of offering large sums of money as a means of investment to support an idea or business venture and help it be successfully launched.

Your immediate reaction might be, "Why would a wealthy person or a business agree to take a chance with someone else's idea?" The simple answer: to earn more money, of course. People are constantly counseled to "invest" their money. This goes for anyone, whether they have $1,000 or $1 million. When you have money, it is smart to invest it in profitable vehicles that will earn even more money than you originally put in. Investors know quite well that it takes money to make money, and they are not afraid to take a chance if they feel their risk has the possibility of success.

There is another option that has become available to the entrepreneur, which piggybacks on the idea of OPM. It is a phrase that has gained popularity over the past few years: OPR, which stands for other people's resources. While it is a similar concept to OPM, the main difference for an OPR source is that an investment of hard cash is not expected. Rather, the OPR investor offers their available resources to help a business get on its feet; these resources can come in various forms. For example, you may be developing a product that you need to distribute, but you have not yet formed a relationship with any distributing channels. So, you form a relationship with a more established company that also has long-established relationships in the area where you wish to do business. Or, you need to manufacture a product, but you do not yet have the capital to purchase a manufacturing facility. So, you enter a contractual relationship with a company that does have a facility, coming to an agreement as to how they will benefit from this venture — such as a portion of the profits.

This is especially attractive to investors because they will not have to pull from their available cash reserves and therefore are not risking as much. For entrepreneurs, this should be thought of as going straight to the source for what they need, rather than asking for money that would be going toward the same resources. The resources are paid for, rather than using OPM to purchase those resources.

When you decide to take the big step into the role of entrepreneur and carry through with your great business idea, there are only two directions in which you can go in order to get that business idea moved from the creative environment of your imagination and out into the marketplace. To help determine which of these choices is better for you, look over your individual situation and list the benefits and costs associated with each one. *Chapter 4 will look more in-depth at the benefits and risks of OPM in particular, since that is the primary focus of this book.* The following overview will help you weigh all of your options:

Using Personal Assets (Self-funding)	
Benefits	Costs
You will not have to give up an interest or any profits in your company. Self-funding means you have fast access to funds.	You risk your personal assets by mixing them in with business. Startup and operations may be limited by the amount of funds and resources at your disposal.

| Using Other People's Money ||
Benefits	Costs
OPM offers you access to greater amount of funds. It can provide you with the ability to speed up the startup or growth timeline.	You take the risk of possibly having to give up a partial interest in your business. You will possibly find yourself having to answer to an investor regarding business decisions.

| Using Other People's Resources ||
Benefits	Costs
You gain access to other's expertise. You benefit from the use of existing strong relationships built by someone else. The resource could include access to equipment or distribution venues.	You may have to give up partial interest in your company.

So how do you decide among them? The answer depends on your particular situation, which includes your goals and the timeline you wish to see implemented. Your situation will be different from someone else's. You may have a greater stomach for risk than the next person, or you may want to move faster in launching your business than someone else might be ready to do. Measuring your comfort level with how you want to handle your business, as well as the level of risk you can feel at ease with, will help you determine if you will use one, two, or a combination of all three of these options.

For OPM in particular, there are three main issues that must be addressed for any large-scale business idea to be developed through the use of OPM. The entrepreneur must:

1. Be able to find a source that believes in his or her idea and is willing to fund it.

2. Be able to meet the investor's criteria for loaning the money.

3. Have agreed upon a price to be paid to the source for the funding.

Using someone else's money is a lot more personal than using their resources, though you will want to have a solid plan if you are going for those, as well. A business person may be offering their reputation as part of the deal in helping you out with their resources, so they will have concerns about your venture and want to know that you will represent them well.

Whether you use your personal assets, OPM, OPR, or a combination of these, there will still be a need for you to invest the time and effort to make your dreams a winning reality.

Types of Businesses

The vehicle that carries your dreams to the reality stage can take various shapes. There are a limitless number of business ideas that can be launched using other people's money. What you will have to do is use your imagination, watch trends, and do the research to confirm the ability of your dream to fly.

Some entrepreneurs have created a new product that solves a problem, which can be traced back in early history to the invention of the wheel or method of making a fire, for starters. For these purposes, consider products that are invented or created to help their inventor build wealth through solving a problem for others. For instance, how about the Weed Eater®? It was invented by George Ballas. He wanted a nicely trimmed lawn but could not get to those tight areas with his lawn mower. So he created a piece of equipment that could, and a product and a company was born — and a problem was solved for millions of homeowners. Other entrepreneurs invent products that advance technology in some way, such as cell phones, which have come quite a long way since their debut in 1973. These entrepreneurs need the means to develop those products that take advantage of technologies as they emerge and blossom. Still, other entrepreneurs like the idea of a turnkey approach to owning their own business, so they want to purchase a franchise to accomplish that end. A turnkey business is one in which you purchase the rights to use the ideas, methods, advertising, and name recognition of an established business. For example, SUBWAY® Restaurants, a sandwich shop that can be found across the globe, was the No. 1 franchise of 2009, according to *Entrepreneur* magazine. If you purchase a Subway franchise, you are going with a company brand that most people recognize. The sandwiches and other offerings are the same across the company, so you are also purchasing an existing means of doing business and can model your franchise off other successful sibling locations.

And there are scores of other entrepreneurs who are searching for a way to fill the demand for a service or develop a service that will soon have a high demand by consumers and businesses. This is where the savvy entrepreneur watches trends. For example, when the Internet first gained a toehold in our collective imagination, there were few companies. Then a groundswell of entrepreneurship occurred: There were dot-com companies being launched everywhere, cashing in on a growing trend and filling these entrepreneurs' personal coffers. The key is having a good exit plan for the business, discussed more in Chapter 7, in which you have preplanned a strategy to get safely out before the bubble bursts. Another example of filling a need would be the rise of personal services, such as personal chefs, personal shoppers, and professional organizers. These enterprising business people saw a trend for people leading extremely busy lives who need assistance in managing it all.

Regardless of *what* your dream is, you can be assured that there is a way that many smart entrepreneurs have successfully employed to make their ideas come to fruition. You may be surprised at some famous names who have used OPM to reach their successful business status.

People who have successfully used OPM

When you think of a "wealthy person," there are some names and images that may immediately come to mind. Odds are, those people employed OPM to launch their ideas in order to attain that high level of financial success. These were bold people who had ideas they wanted to develop, and they found the means to accomplish their goals — with the help of OPM to make it happen.

- **Warren Buffett:** Billionaire investor Warren Buffett worked from the time he was a child. Using money received from family and friends, plus his own investment of $100, he formed a limited partnership at the age of 26 and began building his fortune through investment partnerships.

- **Donald Trump:** Real estate developer and master deal-maker Donald Trump used the concept of other people's money to build his empire, taking advantage of a city program to rehab properties that had fallen into disrepair.

- **Bill Gates:** Software genius Bill Gates saw a coming trend: home computers. His goal was to see a computer in every home — with his software on it. He aligned his small company with the much larger IBM, successfully contracting to exclusively provide software for them, gaining access to a market that he would otherwise have had to struggle to break into.

- **Sheldon Adelson:** Casino mogul Sheldon Adelson got his business start as a pre-teen with a $200 loan so he could deliver newspapers.

Each of these people created great wealth and are the names that people use as examples when referring to the super-rich. But these wealthy people did not just reach into their own pockets to get the funds they needed to begin their business enterprises: They tapped those who had deep pockets and were willing to invest. They dreamed big, then got others to back their ideas and invest money in them.

Immigrants have successfully used the idea of OPM. Some communities, such as Asian, African, and Hispanic communities, for example, have banded together to create funds to help other immigrants within their community open new businesses. It is a tradition that continues because it has worked successfully. Think how much faster the idea of the American dream can be achieved for people new to the United States with that sort of financial backing and support — and, for many of them, while they are trying to deal with learning a new language and culture shock. This is how so many people are able to come to the United States and be successful despite language and cultural barriers: They have tapped into the power of OPM.

CASE STUDY: TRANSWORLD BUSINESS BROKERS, LLC

Transworld Business Brokers, LLC
5101 NW 21st Avenue; Suite 300
Fort Lauderdale, FL 33309
(754) 222-3109
Andrew Cagnetta — Owner/CEO

I think the first time I heard about the concept of OPM and what it could do for me was from a friend as a kid. He opened a business with some investors, and he used the term OPM.

I opened a business right out of college. It was a cell phone store. I bootstrapped it, not realizing what level of working capital was really needed. Next, I borrowed money from my mom to buy a gourmet food business with my cousins. We eventually sold it and repaid everyone. I waited several years until I borrowed more money.

When I first began the process of using OPM, I always feared losing the money. In the case of my mom, I was fearful of losing what she had saved. With my current company, Transworld Business Brokers, I borrowed money from my father-in-law, Joel. I feared that if I lost that money, I would lose not only the money but also the business and my wife (or at least the great relationship I had with her parents). And I am not sure you ever lose the fear. If you do, then perhaps you have no intention of paying it back. But if you believe in your business model, you have fewer concerns.

I would advise the entrepreneur who would like to use OPM to remember that business is business: Put *everything* in writing. You must document what you are borrowing, what the consideration is, and the terms for repayment. There seem to be arguments if either you do well or you do lousy. Plus, you need to borrow enough to cash flow the business *and* yourself; it seems everyone forgets you need to eat while you grow a business.

OPM helped me get into and grow my business. Without it, Transworld could not have taken the risks necessary to execute our growth plans.

CASE STUDY: TRANSWORLD BUSINESS BROKERS, LLC

When it came to finding sources of OPM, well, you have heard the term friends, family, and fools. I guess everyone initially draws from those categories. I moved to Florida at the urging of my father-in-law. (Growing up and living in New Jersey through all those winters, it was not a hard sell.) We had spoken about what I wanted to do in life, and I told him I wanted to get back into business for myself. So he offered to back me if we moved closer (my wife was pregnant at the time). I did ask him to put it in writing, which he did.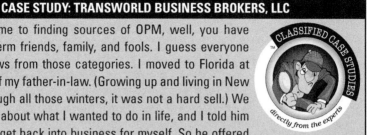

We moved into my in-law's house, and I started looking for businesses to buy. I eventually ran into Transworld Business Brokers during my search and eventually decided to join the firm, thinking if I found a good business elsewhere to buy, I would eventually leave. Two years later, after a short but successful sales career, I bought the company using the loan from my father-in-law. To this day, I think he was crazy, though he says it was the safest investment he ever made. Transworld had seven people at the time, with 35 listings. Three months in, I ran out of money and had to ask for more from my father-in-law. That was not a good day. But he gave it to me, and we scraped along pretty well until 1999.

In 1999 my friend and his partners launched a company that invested Certified Capital Company (CAPCO) funds in New York. They were awarded a CAPCO contract in Florida and needed to invest $12 million in small businesses quickly. We had kept in touch while he was on Wall Street, thinking that someday we would do a deal. He was working on huge deals, while Transworld was brokering small deals. But the CAPCO was to finance small deals. So they visited Florida. We of course showed them as many as we could, but there were no matches. My friend had the idea during one lunch meeting that they should back Transworld. I did not think we needed any money, but when they proposed $3.5 million — that caught my attention.

With that money, we:

    a. Hired top talent.
    b. Advertised globally and locally.
    c. Tripled our office space.
    d. Expanded our geographic reach.

By 2003, we had paid back the money. We were one of the most successful CAPCO companies, putting more than 70 people to work, and sold hundreds of companies that created thousands of jobs. Transworld eventually:

    a. Grew from 10 people to now 85.
    b. Grew from under 100 businesses for sale to almost 2,000.

CASE STUDY: TRANSWORLD BUSINESS BROKERS, LLC

c. Grew from one office to now nine offices statewide.

d. Acquired four other business brokerages.

e. Started or acquired several businesses.

When using OPM, you need leverage (capital) to be successful in business. Very few can build a huge business without OPM, and even if you have the money, often most entrepreneurs will leverage their own money to build businesses anyway.

I have many people who have invested in me, and most are extremely happy they did. I am wildly protective of them and think of them as family (if they happen not to be). To ensure that your investors are satisfied with the relationship, I recommend you properly set expectations. I believe in under-promising and over-delivering.

A new entrepreneur should expect questions when working with an investor — pointed ones. Be prepared and write a plan. For my gourmet food store, we wrote a business plan for the family members who invested. We were clear that the money was a loan, and what interest rate would be paid (12 percent...ouch!)

What will make the bottom-line difference when you go to your OPM source to sell them on your idea is trust. Everyone who has ever lent me money trusted me with their lives — and obviously their money. Never violate that trust.

Chapter 2:

Getting from Vision to Reality

Fine-Tune Your Idea

You have been encouraged to dream big for a reason; if you fall even halfway short of your original intention, you will still land pretty far up the ladder than if you had taken an extremely conservative approach. Look at Bill Gates, for example. What if he had thought "one computer in every state," rather than one in every home? The dream would have been squelched before it could be adequately born, and also would not be as inspiring.

And that makes it an even more important reason to dream big. People with money to invest want something — whether it is an idea, service, or product — that they can feel passionate about, too. They want to be sold on why they should part with their cash to invest in your idea — and how it is going to bring them the return they want for their investment.

> **$ Investors' Insight:**
> A successful idea has one very important characteristic: It sparks passion in *you*. You will need this passion in order to persuade others regarding the strength and potential of your idea. If you are unable to get behind your own idea with heart and soul, then you will be hard-pressed to convince other people to get behind it, let alone give you money for it.

People want to be inspired by big ideas they can support; they like the latest, greatest, and freshest ideas of tomorrow — the kinds of ideas that are considered to be cutting-edge. This is why there is a whole area of research and study that follows what are called market trends. It is a way to keep track of the pulse of what is inspiring people to act now in making purchases, changing their opinions, or moving in new directions.

Investors especially are drawn to fresh ideas. A new vision for a product or service can mean a huge return on their investment. But these investors are savvy — and they will need a good deal of convincing to invest in *your* idea. You will do your convincing of these investors through the use of facts and figures. We will go over how to rein in all of the details of your idea and present a clear, winning picture of what it is you are planning to accomplish, through the creation of a business plan. *This will be covered in detail in Chapter 7.*

Moving From Vision to Solid Business Proposition

How you have handled your personal finances will likely have an impact on your business aims, affecting everything from whether you can qualify for a traditional loan to the amount of interest you will be charged for that loan.

Take stock of your personal assets

Before you get ready to convince others to invest money in your idea or venture, you need to know the most current state of your personal finances. It is time to calculate your assets and your liabilities to see what personal funds you may already have available to tap.

Certainly, you could build an entire business with OPM, but there are pitfalls and costs that may make it more worthwhile to invest your own personal capital before you seek out anyone else's. *Learn more about this topic in Chapter 4.* There are benefits to this approach, such as not having to pay interest or share ownership, not having anyone question your decisions, and most importantly, not having to worry about security laws.

In addition to these, you may want to begin a business using your own capital if:

- You were unable to obtain OPM during the first round of efforts, and time is a commodity not to be wasted in starting the venture. Again, this is an individualized decision, based on your idea and how fast you want to get it moving. If you feel it is something that cannot wait for the right investor to come along and help fund, then it may make good financial sense to use your own capital, if you have some available. It does not make business sense to watch your chance at starting a business float by as you wait for an investor who is ready to back you. *What to do in a situation where you are being declined OPM will be covered in more detail in Chapter 6.*

- You have decided to build up your business first, creating a solid record of success and upward momentum. By building the credibility of the business before going to OPM sources, you will have a better chance of maximizing access to available funds in the future. Investors will not be as likely to hesitate in joining their funds with a company that has a solid track record because, naturally, everyone wants to be involved with a successful venture. Having proof of the viability — and profitability — of an idea will make an investor feel more at ease in parting with his or her money.

Your assets will also come in handy if you are thinking of borrowing from the conventional sources of OPM, such as banks, credit cards, and other forms. These sources will look at your balance sheet, especially your assets, when deciding how much they can risk giving you. In general, the more assets you have, the more money you will be able to borrow.

The basic sources of equity that most people acquire within their lifetime and can draw from for capital are real estate, stocks, bonds, and an existing business.

Real Estate

Real estate can be a significant source of money if you keep your expectations realistic. For the past several years, many investors became drunk with the seemingly easy money that could be made in real estate. They counted on their ability in knowing how to play the system. But similar to the dot-com bubble, the real estate bubble was bound to burst, and the cash-mad idea of "playing the system" is reverting back to the traditional line of thinking: looking at real estate as a long-term investment.

This is not to say that there will not be instances where you can quickly move a home. It is being done, but it takes more ingenuity than simply planting a "For Sale" sign in the yard. After the collapse of the real estate market, everyone is now watching for signs of rebirth. There are investors who look at this collapse as a time of opportunity, and they are taking advantage by snapping up properties for a fraction of the overblown prices seen just a couple of years ago.

You can make money in real estate several ways. One method is to borrow money to improve upon a property, sell it for enough to pay off the loan, and pay for repairs and upgrades, which leaves you with a nice profit after giving the loaner a relatively small fee (interest) for his or her role in the process. This is commonly known as "house flipping" and is one way investors increase their wealth. Currently, the ability to flip quickly has slowed down considerably, and those who got caught on the outside of the boom are now holding properties beyond the timeframe they were expecting.

Besides house flipping, personal property can also be used to boost your wealth through selling, renting, or using it as collateral for a loan. If you currently own your residence or other property, equity may exist on a first mortgage that can be used as capital with which you can invest in a business venture or yet another property. The value of that equity hinges upon whether you have paid your bills on time, if the property is in a good location, and if there is a difference between the current market value as compared to your principal mortgage balance. Many have watched the equity value in their homes seemingly drop, but this is the market righting itself to reflect a truer assessment of the property's value.

Currently, rates are reasonable, so the once-feared words "second mortgage" should not create fear at all. Some people would view a second mortgage as yet another albatross about their necks. A savvy investor knows differently: It is a source of money with which to invest in other ventures and build wealth. There is also the possibility of refinancing your first mortgage, which has become quite popular in recent years. It works in your favor to refinance in an amount greater than the principal balance of your original mortgage and receive the extra cash.

Besides a second mortgage, you also have the option of opening up a home equity line of credit (HELOC). If you have equity in your home, you can open a line of credit for a portion of the estimated value of your home. That line of credit can be used to help fund your business venture and is paid back at a typically generous interest rate.

There are also many variations of real estate acquisition that are available to the imaginative entrepreneur. As laws and technology change, new opportunities open for entrepreneurs to use real estate in new and innovative ways with which to create wealth. *A more in-depth look at real estate as an investment vehicle will be found in Chapter 11.*

Financial Portfolio

There are other personal assets you may not have thought of using that can be tapped for investment purposes. These include stocks, bonds, and life insurance policies. You have been pouring money into these vehicles over time and built a financial plum ripe for the picking — and profit making.

Stocks

Stocks are traditionally the most powerful performers of the three financial-portfolio options over the long run. Rather than a represented debt as with bonds, stocks serve as an equity stake within the business it was bought. Returns from a good stock can raise a steady gain of capital, but sometimes it may be worth more to sell and invest the money into something else — such as your idea. Stocks are no more of a guarantee than the meteorologist telling you today will be sunny. As financial history shows, stocks trend up and down, as witnessed most recently in the 2008 economic downturn. Many stock portfolios took quite a blow. However, over the long run, stocks show more overall gain than other financial vehicles. Stocks are a combination of when preparation meets opportunity, and timing plays a large part as well.

Similar to a new business venture, investing in stocks offers no guarantees of success. Think of it like a poker game: No one has a non-stop winning streak; statistically, at some point, you will lose one or more hands. So, do not feel you are taking an unnecessary risk by using this money, unless you do not have confidence in your business idea. And if that is the case, you should not look into the idea of OPM, either. This is why you have engaged in the exercise of dreaming big: to make sure you have a viable idea that you can get behind and stomach the inherent risk that any new venture brings. Using the equity you get from your stocks to invest in your business idea may bring you more returns over the long-term than if you left them to the vagaries of a sometimes-fickle market.

Bonds

Bonds are a great source of cash for the investor, as they are one of the most steady, secure sources of income you can buy. A bond is a loan for an amount of cash to a company, government, or individual, with the promise that the loaner will receive the loan amount plus interest back from the investor over a set period of years. That is assuming the market value does not drop, or the issuers do not default and can no longer pay toward their promise — in which case, all but government bonds are not secured for the loan amount. From the getting-rich standpoint, bonds do not have a great growth potential unless you have a large amount invested and are receiving a high return. Therefore, more money can be made through another investment vehicle with a strategic business plan in place than with a bond, which would never have the ability to significantly pay out over the average person's life expectancy.

New twist on an old idea: The story of David Pullman

People are always creating new and innovative ways to make more money. One of the most interesting innovators who found a fresh way to use the classic bond would have to be David Pullman, the creator of the "Bowie Bond." Pullman started this phenomenon with David Bowie well over a decade ago, in 1997. He created bonds that are made up of the royalties of a musician's future work and sold them to investors for a set period of 10 years.

This allowed Bowie to receive an early loan, and he did not have to pay taxes on it. This bond was $55 million, and Bowie reportedly used it to buy the rights for the remainder of his songs that he did not already own. Over the course of the 10-year bond period, the royalties came in for his most recent work, and the investors were able to come away with a nice profit greater than what they would have received from a classic bond.

It appeared to be quite the win-win deal, and Pullman left his small firm, went out on his own, and became a Wall Street celebrity. He hung out with musicians and created ties with powerful music executives. It was an innovative idea that he had decided to take a chance on, based on a very basic, "asset-backed" security that he had found a way to market and cleverly create money from.

This shows how creativity can be one of the biggest deciding factors for success. By taking an old idea and creating a fresh twist, a typical entrepreneur such as Pullman can make millions. There will be other innovations like this to follow, and if you are able to be the next creator of such an idea, you could be walking in his shoes. Of course, you are always taking a risk when it comes to such strategic ideas, but this is why everyone is not wealthy. Plus, no strategy and no risk-taking generally equates to no wealth creation.

Over the majority of the time that Pullman has been doing this, he has been in and out of court with Prudential Securities and Charles Koppelman for the alleged attempt to steal his ideas, filing a suit against them in 1999. And in 2006, Pullman was served with a lawsuit from James Brown, with whom he had worked on a similar deal in 1999. He became a laughingstock in New York City for a series of articles in *The New York Times* about his lawsuits and legal struggles with his co-op board. This shows that even the great ideas need to be continually honed and reinvented in order to keep them — along with reputation — protected.

To make matters worse, the addition of the Internet music download trend brought up the question of the longevity of these bonds for music artists, as their albums are not making the profits they once were. In view of this dilemma, Pullman decided to branch out and introduced his intent to use the same technique with intellectual property and entertainment assets, such as writers, where he continues to pioneer his creative idea. This story illustrates the types of questions that you will have to pose upon the creation of such a strategy, such as its longevity and any potential future threats to your idea remaining at the forefront and profitable. Sometimes it is hard to see into the future, but to keep stock in your idea, you are going to have to plan for all eventualities.

Life insurance policies

You may have access to a life insurance policy that has the potential to be borrowed from for a competitive interest rate that can be used as investment capital. This is an option if your policy has a cash value. If you have more than one policy, you may also opt to cash out completely and use the money to invest in your venture. However, be aware of the cash-out scams known as "life settlements." These scams persuade policy holders to sell their life insurance policy for a greater amount than the cash value of the policy; the premiums continue to be paid, and whomever the settlement is done with eventually collects on the insurance payout when the previous holder dies. The terminally ill and retired are the greatest prey for this scam, but anyone can become a victim of someone looking to take an unethical advantage. Before agreeing on a settlement, you may want to seek the advice of an estate planner.

Another great use for life insurance is to secure your business to your family in case anything happens to you. Once your venture takes off, you may want to put any money that you have taken out of your life insurance policy and put it back in the form of an exit strategy. Exit strategies are often the last thing that a success entrepreneur is thinking about as their business is becoming a success, but it is never too late to start preparing for the future and plan for all eventualities. *This will be covered as part of the business plan in Chapter 7.* A life insurance policy is one of the best ways to plan for what will happen to your business in the case of your unexpected death. The way it works is the business owner and any partners must agree on a predetermined buyer of your business or your share of the business. The policy is then set up to pay that person a predetermined sum of money that will allow them to purchase the business, which will give your family and loved ones immediate compensation.

Tap Your Existing Business

The final asset at many people's disposal is the business in which they may already be working to earn more money for. No matter how much debt your business has incurred, there are a few avenues available for you to take in order to create new cash. Along the same lines as what you will find in real estate, you may have some equity at your disposal. If you have equipment in your business that has been completely paid for, you may be able to borrow against it to receive a loan. This also goes for the business owner who has equity built up within the business itself.

For the individual who owns high-tech or heavy machinery, another option is to find a similar business source that will buy your asset and then lease it back to you at a monthly rate. For example, let us say you own a printing press for your business. You could sell it to a source and then rent it back for its use in your business. This is effective for items of great value that may be important for the weekly activities of your business, but do not generate enough income to necessitate keeping them as a full asset within the business. There may be more important areas where you could invest that money, such as in a larger office in a better location that gives you greater manufacturing capacity and access to a bigger market. What you are doing is leveraging an existing asset in order to have the potential of a greater one.

Perhaps an even better method to use, which will allow you to hold on to more of the asset, is to create a time-share with a similar business. A time-share works when you have an expensive piece of equipment for your business that sits untouched regularly. During the times it is not being used, you could be utilizing it as a means to make extra cash. Sticking with the printing press example, you could be making more money by allowing another business who needs to print material on a semi-regular basis to use it. This will create more money at a gradual rate, but there is also a way to receive a large chunk of funds quickly. Rent its use for a six-month or one-year period with a substantial discount — such as 20 percent — if the business is willing to pay the entire amount up-front. This puts the asset to work for you in creating more capital that can then be used elsewhere.

An actual business can, of course, be used as leverage for the OPM that you need to borrow. The underlying fortunes for the majority of venture capitalists are the various business ownerships they have executed with a given timeframe. The power of an asset that is in the form of a successful business can be limitless if the right entrepreneur knows how to make its profitability work for them to create even more profits. Yes, it takes money to create money, but if you have the business assets to back you, it can be just as good as having the cash in hand.

Credit score

Fair Isaac Corporation, also known as FICO, can be your best friend or your worst enemy when looking for OPM. While you cannot borrow from your credit score, you most certainly will be borrowing based on it. An essential part of reconciling your overall financial portfolio and then moving forward with your venture is finding out your credit score and working to boost it as high as possible.

In relation to your credit, FICO is the yardstick used by your lender to assess the level of risk they are taking by lending money to you. It is composed of three scores, one for each of the credit bureaus: Experian, TransUnion, and Equifax. Your FICO score is based on the information that is reported on your financial history as a living, breathing, and tax-paying citizen. Your score calculation can best be described as being based on a pie graph where 35 percent would equal your payment history, 30 percent equals the outstanding amount of debt that you owe, 15 percent is the overall length of your credit history, 10 percent is any new applications for credit that you have made, and the final 10 percent covers the types of credit used.

To learn your score and see how your financial history looks, you will need to order a copy of your credit report from each of those three credit-reporting agencies.

- Equifax Credit Information Services, Inc.
  P.O. Box 740241
  Atlanta, GA 30374
  www.equifax.com
  (800) 685-1111

- TransUnion
  2 Baldwin Place
  P.O. Box 2000
  Chester, PA 19022
  www.transunion.com
  (800) 888-4213

- Experian
  475 Anton Blvd.
  Costa Mesa, CA 92626
  www.experian.com
  (714) 830-7000

There is also another source to check on your credit report, gathering information from all three agencies at once. You can order one of these combined reports annually, free of charge:

- Annual Credit Report Request Service
  P.O. Box 105281
  Atlanta, GA 30348
  www.annualcreditreport.com
  (877) 322-8228

You are entitled to one free copy per year from each agency, so beware of any companies that are trying to charge you for one.

Some companies will tack on additional services, such as credit-report monitoring.

If you want to know what your credit report looks like over the course of the year, order one from each agency every four months. Once you have received your copies, go over every item very carefully. You are looking for any discrepancies, such as credit cards you never opened or a balance on an account that your records show you paid off. You might be surprised at the number of mistakes you may find.

To improve your score, put together a plan of action that will get your credit cleaned up. One thing you can do is begin paying your bills before they are due. Dispute any late payments on your report. If you have an outstanding debt, call the debtor and make arrangements to get the amount paid. You may find some debtors willing to settle on a reduced amount. Also, report any discrepancies to the credit agencies and follow up to make sure they are removed from your report. From this point forward, you will want to receive updates on these scores, at the very minimum on a yearly basis.

$ Investors' Insight:
Contact your credit-card companies and ask them to lower your rates. To remain competitive, they may negotiate with you to keep your business.

Once your credit history has been reviewed, any issues have been cleared up, and everything else seems right, then it will be time to sit down and look at your available lines of credit. Unlike what some people are told, it is not always to your advantage to combine all of your credit onto just one low-paying card. In actuality, it is usually best to use credit to spread your debt over several cards if you are looking for the best possible FICO score. When looking at your use of credit cards, be mindful that you should not place more than 30 percent of your total available credit on any single credit card, but should spread it out over several. For example, if you have five credit cards at 30 percent of your available line, you should be scored higher than if you had only one card at 85 percent of your credit line. By placing lower amounts of debt on multiple cards, ideally you will be left with a large amount of available credit. This shows that you are managing your debt by not "maxing out" on a card. When you charge a card up to the limit, your score lowers because you now have a higher debt-to-credit ratio.

You may often hear commercials for promoting the idea of "consolidating your debt" with the assistance of a debt-consolidation company. Consolidation can seem like a great idea to save you money if you currently carry multiple high-interest cards, but it can also bring down your score significantly if you are not careful. You are acquiring additional debt by getting a debt-consolidation loan, although it is to pay off other debt. Also, if you choose to close some of your credit card accounts, it can lower your score. It will close off those available lines of credit and make any debt you are carrying look like it is a higher percentage of the total credit available to you than if you left that credit availability open. You need to look at your current financial situation and decide what will help you most in your quest to obtain OPM: a higher FICO score that looks good to creditors — but you are stuck with payments on both credit cards while starting your business — or a lower overall payment on current outstanding debt, but a lower FICO score. A lot will also depend on the flexibility of the terms when it comes to paying back the OPM — whether it is something that you will immediately need to make payments on, or if it is an arrangement where you reach a predetermined level of profit before you need to start repaying.

Do not make the same mistake that many would-be business people make in thinking that credit is not important, and that you can still get a loan without it. Your interest rate for securing that loan will be a lot higher for a low FICO score than if that score were higher. It can be described best as an inverse relationship. A low FICO score portrays you as a higher risk for anyone extending you credit — with the concern being they will not see their money again. Therefore, the cost of that loan is going to be higher as a result to cover the risk they are taking with you.

$ **Investors' Insight:**
The higher your FICO score, the better you look to a person or business that is evaluating whether or not to extend you credit.

Also, how you handle your money gives investors an indication of how you may handle *their* money. Now is the time to show what you are about, and the image you project should be one that an investor can believe in: confident, capable, organized, and good at managing money. Granted, anything unexpected can happen to anyone, creating an unexpected bump in his or her financial road and attacking the credit score. Illness and disability rank high in reasons why people get into financial trouble, where medical bills spiral beyond the person's control and ability to pay them on a timely basis.

More than anything, you want to use your credit reports to know what types of questions you may get and may have to answer when you meet with an investor. You do not want any surprises when you go in to negotiate with someone, so advance preparation will save you from looking like you have not done your homework. Have a working plan in place and ready to show that you are making the good-faith effort to clear up any outstanding credit issues. The cleaner your credit, the smoother your business life will be. People want to do business with other people who can show a history of handling money well.

While cleaning up your credit, do not take rash steps. For example, if you have consolidated your credit card debt and have found that you made a mistake and damaged your FICO score, do not compound the mistake by going out and opening a bunch of new lines of credit to counter your previous actions. Such an action will only drop your scores even lower.

> **$ Investors' Insight:**
> Do not have anyone check your credit unless you are doing business with them, because inquiries count against you, which in turn lowers your score. If you already know your score, you can tell potential lenders to, "Base the quote on a FICO score of X." You can also show them a copy of your report. But until you are sure you want to do business with them, there is no need for them to go in and check it themselves.

So far, we have just been speaking about personal credit, which is very important, but so is corporate credit. If your FICO scores are poor, it does not mean your business dreams are now on permanent hold. If there is no possible way to salvage your score enough to get a decent rate, or if you do not have any credit to speak of because you have never borrowed anything before, there is yet another route you can take: borrowing from someone else's credit. This is a creative solution to get you around the credit issue. *This will be further discussed in Chapter 8.*

CASE STUDY: GET RICH WITH ROBERT

http://getrichwithrobert.com
www.greatbonusoffer.com
(888) 302-8018

Robert Shemin — Real Estate Guru and Author of
How Come THAT Idiot's Rich and I'm Not?

All businesses can benefit from the use of OPM. Most entrepreneurs and business people do not get into business because they do not have enough money or working capital — that is the biggest stumbling block. I hear that all the time: "Robert, how do I get started? I have a great idea, I want to do investing, I want to start a business, I want to do real estate, but I do not have any money." The thing is that everybody thinks that they have to do everything themselves, when the beauty of a smart business person is that they let other people do what they do best, while they do what they do best.

For instance, if you have a good idea or business concept that you would like to pursue, it is recommended to focus on that idea rather than the money initially. You may be asking yourself at this point, "How is an idea going to bring me money?" With OPM, the idea gains the attention of the investor, who in turn puts money into your hands to make it a reality. If you were to try to do everything yourself, which I strongly advise against, you would not only have to play the part as the idea person, but also the money source. This is enough stress and responsibility to dishearten even the most confident of entrepreneurs.

Confident or not, almost every successful entrepreneur has used OPM in some form in order to have achieved the status that they have. Only the very lucky are handed millions of dollars to invest and play with. The rest of us must achieve wealth through what we are given, which is sadly very little in the beginning. The only way around the dilemma of not having enough financial backing to start a business is to borrow the backing from someone else. That is what I do in almost every business that I am involved in — I never, ever use my own money.

Once I have a really good business idea, I go to the people with good credit, let them put up the money, and in return I work on the business, which is what I do best. In a sense they become a partner, but they are really more of a "money partner" because they do not usually engage in too much of the business affairs other than providing the necessary funds. So who are these people from whom you can borrow? If you think about it, I bet you can come up with at least one who has a sizable amount of money, or at least good credit. It could be a relative, boss, or friend of a friend — money is always looking for a good idea.

CASE STUDY: GET RICH WITH ROBERT

If by chance you cannot think of anyone close to you, the Internet has really become a great tool for OPM. There are specific sites where an entrepreneur can search out money for their ideas. There are also Web sites available for business loans and small loans, such as Prosper.com. The Web has become a simple yet effective tool for obtaining OPM.

If you talk to a thousand successful business people, they will all say the same thing: Never give up control. How would you like to ride on the back of a motorcycle that goes 200 mph? Most people say they do not want to do that because they are not in control — you want to drive. So even though I may give up some ownership, I recommend always keeping at least 51 percent.

When it comes to pursuing a business venture, one of the worst things is losing your money. The only thing worse is losing someone else's money. To prevent this, you should have a good business plan that has been thoroughly tested, and a backup plan in case the original plan falters. A cushion is also incredibly important. The No. 1 reason that businesses go out of business is not that they are bad businesses. They do not have enough cash flow, so I monitor my cash flow every Friday. I track my accounting, bookkeeping, and cash flow for all my businesses once a week to make sure that they are working. If there is a problem, I want to know about it. Most entrepreneurs do not know until six months too late.

If your FICO scores are poor, all is certainly not lost. I could not borrow $100 when I first started my business, so I went to a friend of mine, Bob, who had great credit. He went to the bank and borrowed the money, and I split some of the profits and revenue with him. It was a win-win.

Debt is stressful, so a lot of businesses in debt give equity, a part of the business, in exchange for capital credit or money. So, instead of paying them money, which would use up my cash or my credit, I will see if they will become partners in my business. This is how I got started in my real estate business. In the last 18 months, I have personally bought or been involved with more than 400 properties. About $80 million to $100 million is in real estate, but it did not start that way. My first deal was one duplex worth $50,000 for $30,000. I went to the bank to borrow the money; I had about $500 in my checking account. The lender could not even let me borrow $50.

So, I went to my friend Bob, who had good credit. Because of his credit, he borrowed 100 percent of the money, and we bought the duplex for $30,000 and spent about $5,000 fixing it up, all on borrowed funds. Since Bob had the loan, and I owned the property, we would split everything 50/50. Each month the rent would

CASE STUDY: GET RICH WITH ROBERT

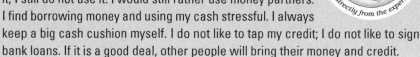

come in, and we would pay the bank loan. I sold it in two years for about $120,000. We paid off the bank loan of $35,000 and split the rest. I made about $30,000 to $40,000 net profit.

Fourteen years later, even though I have the money and credit, I still do not use it. I would still rather use money partners. I find borrowing money and using my cash stressful. I always keep a big cash cushion myself. I do not like to tap my credit; I do not like to sign bank loans. If it is a good deal, other people will bring their money and credit.

Chapter 3:

Sources of OPM

Lending Institutions

There are four different institutional lenders that you will have to choose from: commercial banks, credit unions, savings and loans, and commercial finances.

Commercial banks

A commercial bank is one of the most common forms of OPM that most people are already aware of or have actually used for a loan transaction before. Some people will tell you that bank money is OPM, while others will tell you that bank money is really your own money. This argument starts because they see borrowing money from a bank as borrowing against your own funds. For the purposes of this book, however, OPM is considered any money borrowed to use to support your business plan that — if you did not secure it from some outside source — you would not otherwise have.

The general thought is that commercial banking is the best place to get a business loan. One of the reasons is that commercial banks are insured by the Federal Deposit Insurance Company (FDIC) and typically have the largest selection in institutions with which a business owner can work. It is also generally true that you will have your best chances of getting a business loan through a commercial bank. A commercial bank stands to gain money from a successful business and will not turn away one that they feel will offer a minimal risk with the potential of providing a maximum gain. They are in business, too, and are looking for smart deals to take part in.

Commercial banks offer a variety of services that include checking accounts, certificates of deposit (CDs), loans, and fiduciary services where they will hold something in trust for another, taking responsibility for its care for the other's benefit. They also accept pay drafts and can issue the business letters of credit when they are needed. Beyond these traditional loan services, today's commercial banks also offer credit cards and mortgages to further boost your chances of obtaining funds and allowing you to spend those funds efficiently. The larger of the commercial banks are usually the better option for business. They can offer more perks — such as reduced fees, as well as more local and national branches, and their ATM services are often free no matter where you may find yourself in your travels.

When you are approaching a bank for the first time to ask for a loan, it is almost always better for you to start off with a relatively small deal. You may think that you have found the deal that is going to make you millions, but the bank will see the chance of this coming to fruition as being placed somewhere in the neighborhood of slim to none. Think of your first deal as something that you can easily manage, be successful at, and turn around quickly. It will provide you a foundation of strength for future

ventures and give you a lot more negotiating power for those larger deals.

During the preliminary portion of your OPM acquisition, it is also a good idea to take a deal to the bank as a practice exercise. This is especially good because a banker will tell you exactly what he or she needs in order to make the deal happen. There is no ultimate manual out there that can be found to tell you everything about how to put together a package to present to the bank. Sometimes the best way to learn is through your initial mistakes and the gentle guidance of someone who is hopefully your bank ally. You may have to hear the word "no" several times before you will actually understand how to get to a "yes." Also, the economy and business practices are fluid, changing to keep up with current events, as most recently seen with the housing bust that began in 2006.

$ *Investors' Insight:*
What may have worked last year can change tomorrow based on other business entities, such as banks, working to stay afloat, changing their policies and procedures that can affect your getting a loan.

Regardless of what is going on in the business climate, the best thing you can do is to do your research and create a plan based on what is going on in your market at the current time. There are different market types to be aware of when preparing to approach a bank for a loan: low, high, recession, and recovery. No matter which market you are in, though, banks want to see some basic guidelines met. They do not engage in risky loans simply because it is not their business model. If you or your venture looks to be a risk, they are likely to pass, regardless of the market. The following will increase your chances of securing a loan:

1. **Credit:** Banks follow a traditional pattern of loaning money: If they give you a loan, they expect to be paid back with interest. They gauge your ability to pay them back by your credit history. If you have a history of paying back your debts, they will look more favorably on giving you a loan because you have a history of taking care of your financial obligations.

2. **Collateral:** If lending guidelines are tightening, you may consider offering up something of value as collateral for the loan. This is a step to consider closely before going through with it, though. You need to ask yourself if you are ready to hand over your house or boat, should the business be unable to repay the loan.

3. **Cosigning:** Depending on your credit history and any other factors a bank pulls into the equation, they may only feel confident in giving you a loan if you have someone cosign the loan.

4. **History:** If you have a history of doing business with a bank, they may feel more confident in working with you. Also, if you have a history of owning a business and can show a track record of success, they may also breathe a little easier in extending a loan to your new business venture.

The tighter the market, the tighter you may find a particular lender's guidelines to be. For example, in a recession, the reins of lending can be pulled in, with loans being issued in a trickle. It may be difficult for anyone to get a loan — even those with excellent credit. Banks have their own goals and bottom lines to protect, and their guidelines will remain fluid to protect their own interests. Lending may become so lean, you may have no choice but to seek OPM from non-traditional means, which we will be covering throughout this book.

A good business plan will give you a clear understanding of some of the main features of what comprises a solid business plan; sometimes all a bank really needs is a one-page summary. *The necessity of a good solid business plan will be discussed in Chapter 7.* This short, one-page summary should at least offer what the business will entail, how the money will be used, and who will be running the business; then, everything must be backed up with proof of how the plan is guaranteed to work and pay off. This is especially true if the deal you are working on is relatively small in size and can be easily managed.

You will find there are generally two views regarding relationships with commercial bank lenders: those who believe in using only one faithful bank, and those who believe that you should have no fewer than three to five good, solid banking relationships in place.

The faithful banker plan

Institutional lenders are one of the most popular forms of traditional OPM, and they can become a strong ally to those with decent credit. The key thing that you must understand about institutional lenders is they expect your full patronage and will work their best efforts for you if you satisfy all your traditional banking needs through one bank alone. Some banks can be like a jealous best friend; some banks do not like you stepping out with other banks, seeing what kinds of deals you could get, and borrowing money here and there from a number of different sources. If you want a strong ally on your team, pick an institutional lender that you really like and stick with them. Of course, if a really good opportunity comes along, you may want to try to work something out, but in general, your relationship with your bank is like a marriage in that it is best when it is a one-on-one relationship without any third parties stepping in as temptation. Business is business, but you want to conduct smart business with long-term benefits; you do not want to burn any bridges as you grow your venture.

Advantages
A strong relationship with a financial ally who knows you well.
Disadvantages
Limits on the amount that one bank may be willing or able to lend.
High or variable interest rates, making the cost of the loan greater.
A strong relationship may take time to build.
Your bank may close or be swallowed up by a larger bank, ending your carefully honed relationship and leaving you seeking a new one.

$ Investors' Insight:
Many experts will recommend that you find a backup banker. It is important that you tell them that you are actually very happy with your current bank and are just looking to establish a relationship with a secondary bank as part of your business protocol. Most banks will not have a problem with such a situation and will actually see you as a smart entrepreneur who is simply guaranteeing their business will be free of any hiccups should anything happen with their current banking situation. In this scenario, you will not be stepping on anyone's toes, as you are not actually asking to take out a loan but simply safeguarding your business interests.

The "more the merrier" plan

Not all banks are funny when it comes to sharing their customers with other banks, and if they know anything about smart business, they should probably expect it. The major branches have their own specialties and can offer large sums of money to good clients, but sometimes it is the smaller banks that are more likely to do a deal that the bigger banks would shy away from. It is not a bad idea to have as many options at your disposal as possible.

Advantages
A great source for OPM when all others methods have failed.
Disadvantages
You may have an interest rate that is high or variable.
There are limits on the amount that the bank will allow you to borrow.
It may be difficult to obtain money for those with a poor or nonexistent credit rating.

Credit union

A credit union is set up as a not-for-profit, and because of this, they tend to offer much better deals for their patrons. It is a cooperative-style financial institution in that it has members who have partial ownership in the institution. The earnings are actually divided among its members in the form of dividends or reduced interest rates. There are always exceptions to this general set-up, but it is common for a credit union to offer higher deposit rates and lower fees. However, to get these better deals, you will have to pay a membership fee and then join the credit union by opening a savings account and "buying in" to a share of the union. Only a member is welcome to deposit or borrow money in any capacity. This is what makes the credit union traditionally have better rates and fees; it is basically a nonprofit organization with lower operating costs than the commercial bank and is content with much more modest returns.

Credit unions are not all the same, and most are not insured through the FDIC. However, the National Credit Union Share Insurance Fund (NCUSIF) insures all federal credit unions and many of the state-chartered credit unions. NCUSIF is administered by the National Credit Union Administration (NCUA); this is a federal agency responsible for chartering and supervising all the federal credit unions, which are basically owned and controlled by their members as a co-op system. Most credit unions will offer the same services as banks, such as checking and credit cards, but do so under a different terminology. For example, where a commercial bank will use "checking account," a credit union will call it a "share draft account" — same service, different name. But not all of them will have the same services, and the ones that have more limited offerings will also not be as likely to offer the perks like convenient banking hours for those business owners who are working long hours. The best thing to do is look around at the different credit unions available in your area and rate their services and fees in comparison with some of your larger commercial banks.

Investors' Insight:
Get to know your banker. Your banker may not be your best friend, but the more acquainted you become, the better off you will be in just about every way. Creating a strong relationship with your bank also means having a good rapport with the folks who are working there, and none could be more important than the bank's manager. This process should begin long before you ever even begin the process of trying to borrow one dime. Many times, the bank where you have kept your personal finances will be the place where you will want to open up your business account. Hopefully, they already know you, and you have established a healthy and positive relationship with them.

Savings and Loans (Thrifts)

Savings and loans (thrifts) are similar to commercial banks in that they are in it for profit. While most commercial banks can only branch by acquisition, the chartered thrift has more freedom and therefore no limits in terms of waiting to find another bank they can acquire. It is actually cheaper for them to branch out nation-wide, benefiting the business owner with the lowest cost for services. However, one negative of the federally chartered (savings and loan) thrift is that it is limited to 20 percent of assets in a business loan, a rule that remains in place as of the 2002 Office of Thrift Supervision regulatory bulletin.

Commercial financing

Commercial financing is basically a term used to describe an asset-based lending system. In this system, the borrower is required to offer collateral in the form of personal or business assets, such as a home or other property; these assets are then used to secure the loan. The types of assets that you can gain financing on include outstanding accounts receivable, certificates of deposit, bonds, contracts for import/export, purchase orders, existing inventory, major equipment, franchise development, and existing demand for product or service.

It is never too late to begin fostering a positive relationship with a bank, and there are a few steps that you can take in order to accomplish this:

1. Know your bank manager on a personal level, meaning that you are comfortable enough to invite him or her out to lunch or for coffee. They will be more willing to go out

of their way for someone they know on a personal level than someone who has just walked in from the street. Keep in mind that people do business with people they know and like.

2. Bankers are trained to recognize the signs of a snap business decision in need of quick cash. In general, they are not too keen on such requests because they know that the odds are slim that any due diligence has been done to determine the feasibility of the business idea. If you start building the relationship a few months prior to needing the loan, and you throw out occasional hints that you may be in the market for a loan once you get your business plan solidified, it will greatly improve your chances of acceptance. The reason is that they will know that you have had time to consider your plan, and you are probably less risky than someone who has thrown something together quickly and is looking for some fast money to fund it.

3. Instead of selling yourself to the banker, try forcing the banker to sell her- or himself to you. You want the bank to be aware that not only are you presenting to them a great opportunity to work with an up-and-coming entrepreneur, but that you are looking at other banking options as well. You are serious about your business and are selective when deciding who you think will be your best ally during your climb up the mountain of wealth and success. To aid in turning the evaluation away from you and to the bank, try asking the banker several questions during your initial meeting. Such questions might be:

    • How long have they been with the bank?

- What types of clients has the banker assisted?

- What is the bank's reputation in the business community?

- What type of criteria does the bank use for loaning to businesses?

- What is the bank's capital adequacy, asset quality, management, earnings, and liquidity (CAMEL) rating?

This CAMEL reference is basically asking the banker what his or her bank's safety and soundness rating is. This is something that they may hesitate to give out, as it is rarely given out in public. Do not let that deter you in asking. It will show that you are serious about finding a strong bank to build a good relationship with, more so than just obtaining some quick cash. Also, it will show that you know what you are talking about; you have done your homework.

Venture Capitalists

A venture capitalist is someone who is a professional investor. It is their business; it is what they do. They invest heavily in businesses in the hopes of earning a large return on their investment in the shortest time possible. Venture capitalists want to work with companies that are trying to launch into the top ranks as quickly as possible, offering a product or service that a large number of people may be interested in. Venture capitalists could almost use a chapter all of their own due to the nature of the risk. They are out to make money, which is how they became rich in the first place. They are not "angel investors," who offer money to help a fledgling business get started while gaining capital in return. They are in the deal to make big money, and that is where the stakes in such an arrangement go up compared to working with angel investors. *You will meet Josh Estrin in a case study at the end of Chapter 7, who offers more perspective.*

$$ Investors' Insight:
Venture capitalists think big and want to work with businesses that also think this way. This means they want to be able to invest a large sum of money in order to maximize their financial return as well as their time.

You can expect their relationship with your business to be very "hands on," so be prepared for this if you look to a venture capitalist for financial support. Your business venture may be your personal dream, but they will want to share that dream with you. Again, this is their profession, and they like to be involved. This can be seen as a benefit to you as a new company because these investors have a great deal of experience and a network of support that you will have access to as you grow quickly. Also, because they invest large amounts of money, it only makes sense that they want to be close by to keep their eye on things and help steer the business toward success.

Understand that a venture capitalist has only one goal: to get a huge return. The only way venture capitalists can create the best advantage for themselves in helping an entrepreneur is to take the largest percentage as possible of the venture. The problem is that if the entrepreneur is not careful, this OPM source can end up owning more than 49 percent of the company and become the main decision maker. Robert Shemin, whom you met in a case study in Chapter 2, gave his insight regarding this.

It is common for a venture capitalist to have a charter saying that he or she will not invest in anything unless there is at least an opportunity for a return that is 40 to 80 times their investment. With this level of expectation involved, it is easy to foresee the kinds of problems that can be brewing during the growth of any business. These investors expect big results, and they expect them quickly — or they can become rather unhappy just as quickly. Using the venture capitalist as your OPM source may mean you have a partner who is dropping the hammer on you constantly, working to ensure that enormous return on their investment is being created. You have to decide if you want that type of pressure in exchange for the funding, and whether you can handle having someone question your every business decision.

Because timing is everything with venture capitalists, and due to these high expectations, it is always best to be in a position of their asking to be a part of your project as much as you are asking them to be a part. You would do better to build your business as far as you can take it before you invite venture capitalists to get in on your deal. Coming from the decidedly stronger position of a business that is already growing will give you better negotiating power than if your business is one you are trying to start from the ground level.

What to look for

Realistic terms that can be attained are one of the most important factors of any venture capitalist deal. A lot of new entrepreneurs get so excited over the prospects of a successful company that they accept any amount of money on any terms. What they sometimes do not understand is that there is no shade of gray with a venture capitalist — only black and white. You are either making them the profit they asked for, or you are not. They are not interested in hearing excuses or giving you second chances. The minute you sign a deal, they expect things to go just how you described on your business plan and if it does not, they consider that a breach to what you had agreed upon, and you will now have to work on growing your business while dealing with those repercussions.

The timeline you are given by venture capitalists is very important to them. You have to understand that a venture capitalist has to have an exit plan at some point. This is what venture capitalists do. They usually never stay with any one company but instead work with many different companies, build them up, receive a profit, and then move on to another venture. With this in mind, you are going to want to design an exit plan for them that will not leave you without your own company in the end. *This will be further discussed in Chapter 7.* You have to make sure that you have thought of a way for them to exit the business and still allow you to either keep control of the business or sell it and make enough profit to start another business.

You will probably never find a venture capitalist who does not want an exit strategy for at least five years, but some may want an even shorter time frame. The key here is to give yourself enough time to present a profitable exit strategy to them, while still keeping your business intact and profitable for you and your employees. The more time that you can buy for yourself, the better off you will be, so look for venture capitalists who allow the greatest leeway in their expectations of an exit time frame. You will learn what those expectations are when you meet with them and have a better idea of what is negotiable.

Angel Investors

Angel investors are individuals who are high-net-worth investors. They invest in business by looking for the highest return possible to compensate them for their risk. The actual term "angel" is usually misconstrued as a term of endearment for a caring individual who drops in from the sky to make all of your money problems go away and your business succeed. While this may indeed occasionally work out to be the case, the term actually comes from the early 1900s, when it was common for wealthy businessmen to invest in Broadway productions. These investors were referred to as "angels" for their willingness to make a high-risk investment others would shy away from, making those theatrical productions possible. Today, it is more accurate to think of your "angel" as being an experienced businessperson who deals in non-traditional investments that offer the greatest, albeit most risky, rates of return. They generally have strong connections to several industries and know all the ins and outs of business negotiation, including various laws and contract negotiation. These are private investors who are generally wealthy individuals who do not advertise that fact and deal with business people who find them mostly through word-of-mouth.

> **$ Investors' Insight:**
> Despite the shroud of secrecy that surrounds most of their private investments, we can currently estimate there being about 250,000 active angel investors in the United States. Added to these 250,000, there are likely to be about two million more potential angel investors who are just a step away from receiving a business plan that will launch them into becoming a member of this investment crowd.

The angel investor is indeed taking a large risk when they decide to help fund a project. If something goes wrong, or the business fails, they could be out of much, if not all, of the money they lent to the business venture. To compensate for this risk, the angel investor usually asks for a high rate of return on the money lent to the business and hopes for its success so they can collect a tremendous profit. This return may be in the form of a cash reward and bonus, stock and ownership in the company (which equals shares in profit), or possibly in trade for other goods and services that the business can provide the investor. Unlike the traditional forms of loans (commercial banks, thrifts, and so on) that generally deal in smaller loans for the small business, the angel investor prefers to offer large sums of money that can offer them the most rate of return. It is quite typical for the angel investor to supply $150,000 to $1.5 million of a new business's initial start-up costs. Obviously, that is a large sum to dole out to any business, and they expect to profit beyond average expectations when the business deal works out.

What does an angel investor expect?

To get a better idea and a visual of who these angel investors are, the Center for Venture Research at the University of New Hampshire has done extensive research to paint a picture. They have discovered some common generalities that give an average description of these investors. According to these results, below are some characteristics that describe who they are: the typical patterns of investments they share in common, why they reject certain deals, and where they tend to invest their money.

Angel investors tend to be:

- In the age range of 40 to 55.

- Earning an annual income of no less than $90,000.

- Holding a net worth of $750,000.

- College-educated and self-employed.

- Risk takers who are well-aware that one-third of all such investments will result in a loss.

The patterns of investment for an angel investor follow these trends:

- They generally end up investing, on average, $37,000 per venture.

- They accept three proposals for every ten they turn down.

- They desire to invest in 35 percent more businesses than they actually do each year.

The reasons why angel investors reject proposals include:

- They lack information about the entrepreneur who is presenting the proposal.

- They believe the management team is too inexperienced to do what is proposed.

- The equity is overpriced.

- The numbers given for growth potential are lower than what they are looking for.

Where the angel investor tends to invest are:

- In projects fewer than 50 miles away from their home or office.

- In small businesses just starting with fewer than 20 employees.

This last trend should get you started on thinking about who may be in your city or nearby that invests locally. Angel investors are more than likely going to be interested in becoming a part of the business in some way. There could be a number of things that an angel investor is looking for when considering a proposal by a business entrepreneur. Most will want to have, at the very least, a board position. They expect to have weekly updates, official quarterly updates, and be kept abreast of all new obstacles and accomplishments as they happen. While some of the smaller investors prefer less — and some of the larger ones much more — in general, an angel will ask for a 25 percent stake in a business with some securities (stock) in the business, with rights to liquidation funds should it come to the point where the business has failed and there be anything of value left to liquidate.

For their return on investment, the kinds of numbers that grab the attention of an angel investor are a 30 percent return on total investment for the term of five years, with a net income projection of $20 million. It is possible to gain interest with a smaller return, especially with beginning, less-risky investors, but in general it is the very large dollar signs that capture attention. As mentioned before, you need to be thinking big when you sketch out your business idea; this is especially true when you make a proposal to an angel investor. They are looking for large returns over the shortest possible time, which often means more initial investment, and an aggressive and progressive business plan.

Muse or benefactor: The new "angel" investor

Josh Estrin described the muse or benefactor as someone willing to invest money in a project simply out of a need to either be involved in a business or because of some other form of personal satisfaction beyond money. *See his Case Study at the end of Chapter 7.* Fame is a very powerful motivator beyond money, and while many wealthy investors have plenty of money, they may feel they lack the fame and recognition they would like to achieve, or they wish to make a difference in some way because of some other personal motivator. We all should know by now that money does not buy happiness, and many wealthy individuals are searching for something beyond wealth to entertain and enliven them. This may be an important cause, a business opportunity that is a focal point of the news and media, or a step into a creative career or art form they have always wanted to learn about. It becomes a strong motivating factor and something you will want to give due consideration to when putting together your proposal.

The point here is to always be on the lookout for the variety of ways to finance your business ideas — and the motivating factors that may exist behind them. Money and equity are some of the most powerful tools in any business deal, but for some, personal growth and experience can be just as important. A good way to find these folks is to do plenty of research on your business and look up key individuals who may have a great interest in what you are trying to accomplish for personal reasons. Who would be interested in what your business is doing? Look at your product or service and define who it benefits. Then, look for organizations or people who have an interest in that area. Some investors would like to find ways to give back, showing their gratefulness for the good things they have accomplished and acknowledge the help they may have had along the way. This can also include people who have a connection that is highly personal, such as through a family member, a region where they grew up, or a particular cause they favor for whatever reason.

For example, assume you are designing a sensor that will be able to take the place of a guide dog and will provide a safer and more convenient method for the blind to live alone. There are many benefactors who might have had some personal experience that involves a family member or friend who is coping with blindness. They may be drawn to a business deal that they can provide funds in exchange for helping others and being recognized as an important benefactor for a cause they believe in; this is their opportunity to contribute and make a difference. Still other benefactors may have a slightly more ego-driven reason for wanting to contribute, such as the opportunity to attend celebrity events and talk shows in exchange for their funds. Motivation, as you can see, can be spurred on by what brings an individual a sense of satisfaction, accomplishment, or good, old-fashioned profit.

One of the advantages of working with angel investors is that they usually do not have a tight timeline for which they expect things to be happening the way venture capitalists generally will. They can usually find happiness in being part of a successful company for quite some time before expecting any return on their investment. And there are even some who will be happy in never receiving a huge return, as long as the company is bringing them satisfaction and is not *losing* money for them. There are very few "angels" left in the world these days, but sometimes an arrangement can be made giving you the upper hand with your business venture as if you did actually have an angel come down from the sky and place several thousand — or even million — dollars in your hand.

The angels are not so angelic today

It is hard to deny the risk that can be associated with OPM in the form of a wealthy investor. OPM of this nature has always been risky, but some say that today it is even more the case. The business world is filled with high expectations; so much so that even the angels have begun to expect a lot with their investment funds. Many so-called angel investors today are family members, but even they expect a high return and are sometimes harsher to deal with than venture capitalists.

An angel investor is able to build a company up with the use of their kind contributions. Historically, sometimes these investors would make money and other times lose it, and it was always considered to be a bit of a gamble.

Today, this term has spread to mean many different business ventures, and an angel investor is simply an individual who has lots of disposable income and therefore has the ability to put large amounts of cash into something without the worry of being thrown out on the street or going bankrupt if things do not go right. With that said, however, if these people did nothing but throw away their money to every entrepreneur with a grand plan, they would certainly be broke in no time, no matter how much disposable income they may have to play with. For this reason, these individuals are not a free source of cash. They will expect something out of the deal, and it will be up to you to outline exactly what they can expect in return if they decide to provide you the use of their money. Probably the greatest difference in angel investors today is some of them do not have the patience they have had historically. In this respect they have developed the mindset of a venture capitalist and have clear expectations that they want to have met within a certain time.

$ Investors' Insight:
As long as your plan is on schedule and everything you have promised is coming to fruition, any source of OPM can be a pleasure to deal with. But if you expect delays or foresee any problems in the future, this must be something to consider when looking for the perfect source of cash or resources because whomever you join with will be an active voice in everything you do in your business — especially if they front a large portion of money as angel investors.

Joint Ventures

What interest should you have in a joint venture?

Sometimes one of the best ideas for accessing a source of money will be to partner with another business entity. This alliance between the two interested parties is not a merger as such because there is no actual transfer of ownership between the two parties. Instead, it is a decision to share assets, knowledge, market shares, and profits. The companies involved are allowed to keep what is theirs, but they combine resources in a common interest to create potentially more profit than what could be generated individually.

Joint ventures have two primary needs: helping the business learn new technology that will make the company function more

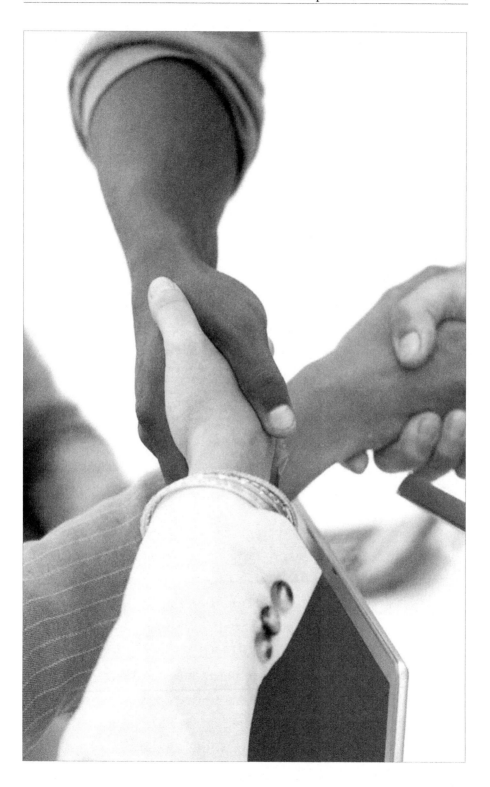

efficiently and enable new markets to be opened to their product that they would not have otherwise had access to. If you are partnering with a large company that is interested in expanding in your operating area, this could mean that you have just found a great source of both OPM and OPR. A joint venture can be a great opportunity as long as you are able to find the right company with which to align your company.

A joint venture can create a rather large business out of a very small one. Sometimes a small business can insert itself into a larger corporation in a market it would like to saturate. The larger business can engage in a joint venture with the smaller company and profit through its success, while the small business can become a rather large force in the market in a very short period of time. Small entrepreneurs need to understand that even they have things to offer that a larger company may want, such as an area of specialty, and if they can convince them of that, it will be as good as obtaining OPM from them.

One problem that can occur is that one of the companies may be afraid to share its technology with a potential competitor, while the other company is afraid to share its market area. If both businesses cannot find a measure of trust between one another, they will not be able to give each other the support they need in order to assure the success of the venture, therefore crippling its potential. Also, a joint venture can mean that while you will be gaining power and OPM within your business-marketing area, you may also lose a portion of the control you have over your business as a whole. In other words, you have to decide whether it is more important for you to own 100 percent of a $1 million-dollar company, or only 10 percent of a $100 million-dollar company.

Not all joint ventures are created equal

Both parties must share equally in order for an initial agreement to work effectively. Such a plan is accomplished with due diligence by checking the credentials of the other business. If both businesses can agree on a fair trade of services, then this is well worth the effort. If the parties cannot agree, then this will only lead to lost money and time — none of which a new business has the luxury of squandering — ultimately defeating the initial intent, which is to strengthen their position.

The key to the acquisition of a successful joint venture arrangement is to find a need that a similar business may have and find a way that you could fill that need for them in a way that can be spelled out within a partnership agreement. Many joint ventures involve the combined efforts of two businesses targeting two different market areas. It is not uncommon for one business in the United States to want to partner with a business in, for example, Asia. This could be a piece of a market that would be very costly to get into without the combined efforts of a couple of businesses that form a joint venture to tackle it.

As good as this can look on paper, it is certainly not a fix-all for a business that is either stagnating or new and looking for an alternative market or technology. Out of 100 such joint ventures, only 40 percent of them will be successful by the end of five years. The other 60 percent would have dissolved long before that five-year period. Do your homework to find a qualified, developed company to venture with, and your chances of success will go up exponentially.

The most important part of any joint venture besides negotiations is the contract itself. Every joint venture you consider must have an agreement so that both parties know what is expected and the parameters of what will be involved. These are generally very standard and straightforward agreements. They are fairly easy to come by on the Internet, but in general, there are a few important aspects you will want to make sure get covered. The biggest concern is in what form payment will take. Will it be cash? Will it be part ownership of the business? Or is there technology your business is producing that the co-venturing partner may be able to use in return? Other aspects to consider is who is responsible for making decisions and operating the business day-to-day; who will be responsible for expenses; and under what terms will the joint venture dissolve.

$ Investors' Insight:
Spell out everything possible in writing, even if it seems repetitious — especially anything that has been discussed verbally, for an understanding to be reached. Do not take for granted that memories will serve either six months or six years down the business road.

Federal Government

Government agencies: There is magic in the SBA

The magic acronym for this section is SBA, otherwise known as the Small Business Administration. State and local government are supportive of small business ventures, as they stimulate the economy for a region because they often create jobs. For all the complaints people have against the government and taxes, they can learn to take advantage of the money they have put into the government and let it work for them. It has become a big help over the past five years because the government has realized that its best chance of getting a return is through the funding of small business programs.

The SBA is not the source for your loan, but rather the coordinator for the loan using a participating bank or institution. When an institution sees a business as unfit or too big of a risk, the SBA will step in and make as much as a 90 percent guarantee to the bank that the loan will be paid off by the SBA, regardless of what happens to the business. This handy guarantee makes banks friendlier to deal with, especially if you are getting used to being turned down. These loans are not handed over to just anyone, however; the entrepreneur must prove through an extensive application process that they will be able to pay off the loan and have collateral to back it up.

The SBA loan is a good option due to its favorable terms as compared to what you may find with conventional bank financing. SBA programs do not require a large down payment, whereas 20 to 30 percent is common for the conventional lending institution. The typical down payment for an SBA loan is 10 percent, and they have the ability to offer an amortized term of up to 25 years. The SBA also does not carry balloon loans that will drop a large bomb on the business once the loan has reached maturity.

Small businesses fall prey to the balloon loans because they are initially attracted to the relatively low payoff amount over the course of the loan. This can be beneficial in terms of managing the cash flow of the business. The problem is if they do not save up for the large balloon payment at the end of the loan, they will be forced to refinance and incur the penalty of several fees on top of their balloon payment. With the typical loan amortization, the time between the initial loan and final judgment day is within five to ten years, which can be a delicate time for most new businesses.

The SBA helps keep money where it is needed — accessible and flowing in the small business — rather than the business depleting all of its own capital, which could potentially result in stifling its growth. These loans are also compatible for small businesses, as well as the moderately small corporations. They offer loans starting from the low-end of the spectrum to $2 million to $5 million. This is not going to be sufficient for a Fortune 500 company, which work with multimillion dollar loans; these programs were not designed for the big guns that small businesses have to sometimes compete against, but they can help level the field a bit. There are eight popular SBA programs available today. To begin, talk to your bank about applying for a loan through them. Again, the SBA does not extend you a loan directly, but rather it works with lenders. You need to supply your bank lender with any paperwork they request in order to submit a loan application, such as financial statements, along with your business plan. If the bank is unable to extend you a loan, ask them to consider your loan under the SBA's guaranty program. Be familiar with the details of all eight of the SBA's programs.

Basic 7(a) Loan Guaranty

This is SBA's primary business loan program. While its maximum allowable loan is $2 million, it is the SBA's most flexible business loan program in its terms and eligibility requirements and is designed to accommodate a wide variety of financing needs. Most of these loans are given to serve functions such as working capital, machinery, equipment, furniture, renovation, new construction, and debt refinancing. Commercial lenders are the ones who actually make the loans and the determination for whom they will loan to, but the government offers a guaranty for a percentage of the loan should the borrower default. For this particular loan program, the government can guarantee up to 75 percent of the total loan made to the business if it exceeds $150,000 and 85 percent for loans less than $150,000.

The most attractive features of the 7(a) is its low down payment, low interest rates compared to most banks, and an extended loan maturity for as many as 10 years for working capital and 25 years for fixed assets. These are great perks. Should a business want to do an early payoff, a very small percentage of the prepayment amount will be charged as a prepayment fee. The early payoff can come in handy when a business is experiencing fast growth and needs to refinance in order to support its expansion, and the small fee required to do this may be more than worth their while.

Microloan Program

This short-term loan offers very small loans up to $35,000 to small businesses that are starting up or growing. Funds are made available to intermediary lenders who are nonprofit and community-based, and these lenders typically require some form of collateral for the loan. The loan can be used as working capital to fund the operations, to purchase inventory, supplies and equipment in order to do business, or furniture and fixtures for the business. There are intermediaries available in most states, the District of Columbia, and Puerto Rico. The states where there is no intermediary include Alaska, Rhode Island, Utah, and West Virginia; Rhode Island and a section of West Virginia are currently accessing intermediaries in neighboring states.

Prequalification Pilot Loan Program

This program allows for a small business to have their loan applications analyzed and receive a potential blessing from the SBA before a lender or institution takes it into consideration. It covers loan applications in which the business owner is looking for funds up to $250,000, and its deciding factor involves aspects of the applicant's credit, experience, reliability, and — to some degree — character. This makes it unique among many of the other loans, where the applicant must have assets in order to be qualified.

The main purpose for the SBA in this particular program is to help the entrepreneur strengthen his or her loan application. This program can be helpful for an applicant who has relatively good credit and a semi-established business looking for expansion. The SBA will ask to see the applicant's past financial records, ratios, history, and personal credit. The SBA will help determine which sections of the loan request are potential red flags for the bank and then recommend the most favorable terms the applicant should expect.

8(a) Program

This program was specifically designed to help socially or economically disadvantaged people (minority entrepreneur or business leader, or person with a disability). These loans are traditionally used for a start-up or expansion business development. To qualify, a socially or economically disadvantaged person — not just a figurehead in the position — must own and control at least 51 percent of the business. Along these same lines are additional assistance programs that are specifically targeted to veterans, women, and handicapped persons.

Economic Opportunity Loans (EOL)

This program is for the low-income business owner, who may be experiencing even more difficulty in securing financing despite having a sound business idea. As long as one business partner is considered to be living below the poverty level (determined by the federal government and adjusted annually for inflation) and owns at least half of the business, an applicant can qualify for EOL assistance. It is also an option for the small business that has already been declined by a conventional bank or institution. The best part of the EOL program is that the loans are long-term and offer a flexible payback rate of 10 to 25 years, depending on the type of loan.

LowDoc Program

The LowDoc (short for low-document) Program is set up to make the application process much simpler, less time-consuming, and quicker than traditional methods. It does this by reducing the size of the application form to one page for loans under $50,000. For larger loans of $50,000 to $100,000, an applicant receives the same one-page application, along with a request for his or her past three years of income tax returns. This program is the most popular in the SBA's history.

CAPLines

A CAPLines loan is an asset-based line of credit, allowing businesses to manage their short-term needs, such as to continue payroll and purchase equipment. Typically, a business that is unable to qualify for other lines of credit, such as a builder or small company, will use this type of loan. The payback terms of a CAPLine are adjusted to fit the seasonality and cash flow of a business, such as a business trying to complete a large project and waiting for payment.

CDC/504 Program (Certified Development Company)

This is a mortgage product that supports local community developments through commercial real estate. The Certified Development Company puts up 50 percent, the bank 40 percent, and you come up with the remaining 10 percent. You must occupy/lease 51 percent of the building, and you are free to lease remaining 49 percent of the building to another business. Also, the business must create jobs, and the more jobs the business creates, the more money will be lent to the business. The terms of a CDC/504 program are attractive, offering a generous, 25-year fixed rate.

SBA lenders are not all created equal. They are separated into three categories, each category participating in the programs with different verve and commitment.

The least helpful in most cases will be your participant lenders. **Participant lenders** are occasional participants in the programs offered by the SBA, which would be your average bank's status. These are known to be slow in processing and often impersonal. They are also not highly trusted by the SBA to determine an applicant's qualifications. For this reason, the SBA checks over each application and will have the ultimate say on whether the applicant meets requirements for the loan.

The next best SBA lender to use would be the certified lenders. **Certified lenders** are considered certified because they are regular participants of the SBA programs. Processing time for these loans is shorter, as they are more accustomed to the processing than participating lenders. While they understand the SBA process better and complete the necessary requirement checks thoroughly, the SBA still insists on double-checking the decisions of the bank before qualifying the loan.

The best type of SBA lender is the preferred lender. **Preferred lenders** know the SBA system and have a solid reputation with the SBA as being a good judge of character and risk. Because of their experience, the SBA trusts them and does not get involved in the decision-making process of acceptance. If the bank accepts the applicant, the SBA is 100 percent behind the decision. This is the quickest and most convenient way to take out an SBA loan.

Grants

So far, we have been speaking about the many forms of government funding that have to be paid back. What if there was a way to dodge this aspect of borrowing money? There exists such an excellent tool for some businesses, known as the grant. Grants exist because things need to get done, and these goals require people in order to carry out the work. They tend to center on projects where people want to help people, and the money is intended for a specific project or purpose. You will need to meet the conditions mandated by the grant-giver, then use the funds for the mandatory purpose. Grants must be applied for, in which you respond to a request for proposal (RFP) and follow the criteria that have been issued as to what types of information is needed for the organization giving the grant to reach its decision. Proposals are reviewed, and the grant money is awarded to the winner(s).

While the federal government is not as generous with its use of grants for most small businesses, many local state governments are. About the only small businesses eligible for a grant these days are research firms in the engineering and scientific areas because these are capable of serving the needs of the country. These grants are through the Small Business Innovation Research Program, which you can check out online at **www.sc.doe.gov/sbir**. Its motto, according to the Web site, says it all: "Supporting scientific excellence and technological innovation through the investment of federal research funds in critical American priorities to build a strong national economy... one small business at a time." Government entities recognized that small businesses were engaging in more innovation than bigger businesses, but the funding had been tilted in favor of those larger companies. This program helps level the field, so small businesses are able to compete and continue to innovate.

Beyond these few choice financing entities that answer the need of the federal government, the small business can find yet another ally closer to home than they may have realized: their state government. Every state has its own rules and privileges, so you will need to contact your state's economic development center. Research their Web site to see what they offer. *A list of these Web sites can be found in the State Resource Web site guide at the back of this book.*

💲 **Investors' Insight:**
Make it a habit to review grant sites frequently. New ones become available all the time. If one grant does not fit today, there may be one next week that will be a perfect match between your idea and the grantor's guidelines.

Government grants are created to fulfill specific purposes and can have very narrow qualifying requirements. You may not find a government grant that you can fulfill, nor are you able to fit within its stringent guidelines. But the government is not the only entity that offers grants. In addition to government grants, there are three more types of grants: foundations, corporations, and individuals.

Foundations: An alternative to government grants is available through the private sector via foundations. There are about 100,000 foundations that may be interested in what you do and might be willing to provide you with the cash to bring your idea to fruition. For example, if your business idea involves an eco-safe cleaning service, there may be an eco-friendly foundation that would be willing to offer you a grant. For more information on foundation grants, go to **www.foundationcenter.org.**

Corporations: Many companies set up programs in which they offer grants or will match money for the development of products and services that match their industry, and sometimes also resources such as their expertise or equipment. Typically, they offer grants to non-profit organizations within their community to show support for local causes. If your business idea is to establish a nonprofit organization, look around your community for existing businesses that are already involved in the type of outreach programs that align with your idea.

Individuals: Generally, wealthy philanthropists set up foundations through which they issue grants. Again, it will depend on your business idea and if it strikes a chord with someone who is interested in what you are trying to accomplish, especially if your endeavor is civic-oriented. Individual grants are very competitive, and the guidelines can be very specific in what the grant provider wants done with their money. So, if you cannot find any grant opportunities through the government, foundations, or other corporate entities, an individual philanthropist could be a viable option. *There is more information relating to grants specifically for real estate in Chapter 11.*

CASE STUDY: SILVER SPOON PERSONAL FINANCIAL OFFICERS

Silver Spoon Personal Financial Officers
6631 Main Street
Williamsville, NY 14221
Phone: (716) 565-0137
Fax: (716) 633-1333
www.SilverSpoonFinancial.Ning.com

Market Domination Magic
Double Your Sales In A Year
Phone: (716) 908-3164
www.MarketDominationMagic.com
Seth Greene — CEO

I first seriously began studying the concept of other people's money, other people's time, other people's customers, and other people's resources when I learned it three years ago from my marketing coach, Dan Kennedy.

My dreams would not have been possible without OPM. Going into it, my greatest fear was not getting the money, and then when I got it, paying it back. I do not fear that any longer. In fact, I am always looking for more now.

I would tell an entrepreneur who would like to use OPM that leverage is a double-edged sword. It works great on the way up and might fall short on the way down — so avoid the way down.

OPM provided the initial start-up capital and ongoing cash reserves for the first year of my business. I located my sources of OPM by personal networking through Business Networking International (**www.BNI.com**) and also on the Internet. I think OPM is a great resource: Why would you want to put your own money at risk if you do not have to? As for the investors I have worked with, they are getting a great return on their investment.

To ensure that their investors are satisfied with the relationship, I would recommend that an entrepreneur be very careful about specifying all the terms ahead of time. Also, have a backup plan: It is a good way to ensure things will not go downhill.

CASE STUDY: SILVER SPOON PERSONAL FINANCIAL OFFICERS

What a new entrepreneur should be prepared to expect when working with an investor really depends on each situation, but try to imagine what you would want to know if you were putting your money in someone else's business. Those are probably the same things an investor would want to know.

When I went for OPM, I feel there were certain things that contributed to my success in obtaining it: Salesmanship, marketing, a proven track record, confidence, and not settling for less.

Chapter 4:

Benefits and Pitfalls of Using OPM

Leverage Your Resources

When a new business idea is being formed, especially during tough economic times, it is even more crucial for you to have the ability to leverage your resources. The leveraging of resources refers to the ability to take advantage of all the positive aspects you have going for you at any one time, whether they be financial or relationships. In terms of OPM, this means all of your current personal resources can be strengthened twofold once they are combined with the resources of that powerful money source. You will be able to employ top workers and cover their paychecks for several months, secure a workable office space in a decent location, and protect your resources by ensuring you have enough money to cover your expenses without putting your personal finances at risk, such as your home, cars, or stocks.

When you are attempting to launch your business idea, the last thing you want to do is risk all of your personal assets. It is one thing to lose everything in a business, but even more devastating if you lose your personal finances with a business crash, as well. OPM can offer peace of mind because you can leverage your resources with this extra money that you would not have otherwise had. Should your business fail, you then only have to worry about repaying the OPM money, rather than figuring out how to live if you have depleted all of your personal resources.

Leveraging your business resources is similar to leveraging your own personal ones, as when refinancing your home or pulling equity out of your home. It is never too soon to begin to think about leveraging the resources of the business you are building or already have established. With those resources, you can take on a new venture or strengthen an existing one.

> **$ Investors' Insight:**
> Sometimes using your equity is worth more than just saving up your money in a 401(k), especially if you are in your early 20s and in the lowest tax bracket. You may be able to use your own resources for greater long-term profit.

Before using your own resources, though, proceed with caution. Look at your resources as having the potential to offer opportunity, but weigh the level of risk you are willing to take with them. Set the criteria for what you are willing to risk, and do not go beyond it. For example, maybe you are comfortable with risking 30 percent of your business assets and just 10 percent of your personal assets. Now, you have a working number to fund your venture or expansion plans, and depending on that number, you will be able to calculate how much OPM you will need to supplement it. You may decide you are not comfortable risking any of your personal or business assets. Again, this gives you an idea of exactly what you are looking to obtain from an OPM source.

Manage business cycle flow

Just like the Archadeck example in the introduction of this book, every business will go through cycles. Because Archadeck is primarily an outdoor structure business, it is dependent on good weather; therefore, there will be many places where it will not be able to build in the winter. OPM would be especially helpful in this example, as it would help to cushion the down cycles and allow the business to continue marketing and advertising, even during the times when there is not a positive cash flow. This will become especially important as the business prepares for the spring, when customers are gearing up for their outdoor projects and starting to scout out companies with which to work. But financially, coming out of a slow season and into a busy one can be difficult for the business. Spring is one of the most important times to advertise in the outdoor construction business, yet after a long cold winter, it can be one of the worst times for a business to spend several thousand dollars. Yet, without several thousand dollars invested, the business will not gain the necessary customer leads to have a fruitful building season and be prepared for the next slow winter cycle. Businesses have to build its operations around the dictates of their market, and that does not always coincide with the cash flow of the operation. The business cycle has to be taken into account and worked into the planning stage. *This will be discussed in more detail in Chapter 6.*

$ Investors' Insight:
When trying to estimate what would be an adequate cash flow for your business, think of it as the "rainy day" fund of your business. What does it take monetarily to keep your business operational for a span of time, such as six months or a year?

Without adequate cash flow, this could lead to an unfortunate chain reaction of bad years for the business that does not have the available funds to put forth a strong marketing and advertising strategy. Business cycles are the norm for any business, but to a new business or idea, it can put an end to its growth before it has had a chance to prove itself. Cash flow is an issue and becomes even more of one during a down cycle. OPM is the perfect way to strengthen a business during hard times and prepare for an upswing of new business, booming profits, and future growth opportunities.

Benefit of Using OPM

Ability to seize business opportunities

It would be great to have a fairy godmother come into our lives every time we had a great idea. She would swoop in and supply all the funds for us to put together the business plan, hire the right people, and begin a full-scale marketing campaign. But anyone who has experienced saving up for something they want knows it can be a painstaking process that takes years. Sometimes, within the initial savings process, we are defeated before our idea can ever take off. OPM can serve as the fairy godmother you have been waiting for to grant your wishes.

Another consideration is the timing of any particular plan. The greatest ideas that make people millionaires are at the forefront of technology before anyone else has thought of them. Imagine if Microsoft Corporation were never given the proper financial backing to market itself successfully. The public would not have the computer software we are familiar with today, but it is more than likely that someone else would have thought of something

similar and stole the hot air right out from under the original thinkers, making scads of money in their place. This is a position none of us will ever want to find ourselves in. Great ideas usually have a time limit, whether it is the perfect time to launch a certain fad or develop an idea before someone else does. There is no time to waste when you are dealing with businesses, ever-changing markets, and the constant flow of new generations of consumers, leaders, and thinkers. Keep in mind that you are not the only one out there looking for opportunities to launch your business dreams and create wealth.

Traditionally, gaining access to OPM can be done through either debt or equity financing. The debt refers to a loan or borrowing of money that can be backed up by either selling bonds or raising capital. Equity refers to the possibility of the OPM borrower selling a portion of his or her ownership (interest) in the venture to the source, making them a business partner. In even simpler terms, debt involves cash being handed over to the entrepreneur to use for his or her business idea. In return, a mutual agreement is formed whereby the borrower must pay back the principal (plus interest), under agreed-upon terms. Equity is when the money contributed to the project becomes a percentage toward the ownership of the project or profit in the business.

Like most things that provide a benefit, there is a flip side to using OPM, which is covered next. You will want to be aware of the pitfalls and weigh them carefully in your decision-making. Deciding to use OPM, either to entirely fund your venture or just a portion of it, will depend on your particular financial situation, the business idea you are selling, and whether you want to be involved with OPM at all.

Pitfall of Using OPM

Interest payments

The most obvious cost an OPM loan will entail is the interest payments. Unless your OPM sources are not interested in making money along with their risk from the investment in your idea, they need to secure an interest payment plan to gain back their money and earn themselves a profit on top of their initial investment. There are many sources of OPM where interest is mandatory, such as bank loans and credit cards. In these situations, it will not matter how great your idea is as much as what condition your credit is in at the time. Having confidence in your presentation will have some weight, but they will be looking at the numbers and the risk level they would be incurring by giving you money. The greater they deem the risk to be, the more interest you will be paying.

There are other reasons that will be the deciding factors on the conditions and rates of a loan, but it is important to understand them and hold out for the best possible offer. This is not always defined as being the lowest interest rate. Every bank has its own policy, but as an entrepreneur who is about to embark upon a new business idea that needs OPM to get a solid start, you should search for a bank that is interested in a long-term relationship. Remember that the hard work and sacrifices you are making so that you can create a successful business will also benefit those who do business with you. In your desire to get OPM, do not lose sight of the fact that you are bringing something to the deal, as well; you are not asking for something for nothing.

As a smart entrepreneur, you must take into account future holidays, cash shortages, special marketing expenditures, and industry cycles beyond that initial loan. You may need money up-front to get things rolling, but you also want to make it clear that this is a venture that may come across a few other bumps in the road where you will need another loan or two to see you through. You want a clear path for future loans available to help your business ideas continue to grow and prosper.

If a bank seems to shy away at the thought of forming a relationship to help you build your dream, then they are not the bank for you. Even if they are offering the lowest interest rate, if they do not seem interested in working with you long-term, then you would be better off taking a higher interest rate from someone who is. While short-term loans may be alluring, it is not necessarily the best way to go if you cannot leverage a relationship for your long-term goals. Keep in mind your long-term goals and constantly work toward them. Do not be tempted to keep under wraps the possibility of needing more money in the future because you fear it will lead to your initial loan request being turned down. The best source of OPM is one who understands what you are trying to build and its growth potential, and one who is willing to take a small part in it as that financial fairy godmother from time to time.

Another aspect of the initial bank interview that you should keep in mind is security funds. Some banks will ask you to leave funds as a form of security — in the form of a savings account, CD, or checking account — in exchange for offering you a lower rate. Do not fall for this trap, as it is not saving you anything by tying up money that you may otherwise need for expansion. The whole point is to have funds *available* to you. In addition, some banks will require a percentage of your loan to be paid to keep your line of credit open for future use. In the end, these tactics are only raising the amount of interest you are paying. Interest rates will vary from bank to bank, but they will not vary enough that you should focus solely on the interest rates. You should also be looking for a solid relationship that offers the possibility of usable open credit.

Considerations When Seeking an Investor

When looking for an investor to work with, keep in mind that it is easy for an investor to walk away from you, but not so easy for you to walk away from the investor. They can decide not to be involved with your business, but they may not leave you the choice of if you care for their involvement. This thought has also been coined as "smart money." You should remember to take money from a source that will add something to your company or idea, rather than because you are desperate for money. When you are excited about an idea and are looking for some quick cash to make it happen, you must ask yourself a few questions: Whom do you want to be working with for the next five to ten years during the build process of your idea? How involved do you want them to be in your daily business operation? Is this a person with whom you feel comfortable building a close, long-term relationship?

The business partner you bring on the business venture, whether they are a silent partner or not, will not go away. By accepting your partner's money, you have attached yourself, your idea, and your company to him or her. You have to make sure you both see eye-to-eye, understand each other's goals, and have a clear idea of what each person expects out of the other. This is important because if a relationship between business partners becomes sour, it can not only wreak havoc on the growth of the idea, but also cause a chain of events that could force you, the creator of the project, to be forced out of the picture at some point.

To fulfill the task of gaining your investor's respect, attention, and confidence, you must be able to qualify your business idea. One of the best systems for gaining respect has been used for decades by Gary Patterson, C.P.A., M.B.A., who has more than 30 years experience with mid- to large-size organization planning. *He shares it in the case study at the end of Chapter 6.*

Sharing ownership of your business

One of the hardest things to do as an entrepreneur is giving up a piece of your company or idea to your money source when they never took part in the actual conception that you went through. This is something you will have to decide that you can live with before you begin to approach sources with your idea. It can be a big selling point for a good idea that the co-venturer believes in, but if you are not willing to part with a percentage of it, then you will not want the thought to cross the table. You do not want to appear uninterested in a partnership in the beginning, as it may be construed as selfish and uncooperative; few want to get involved in business if this is the type of relationship to which they have to look forward.

Be careful to not give away too much of your idea to gain the necessary resources because you risk being taken over by your partners and becoming a distant memory to the business. This phenomenon is common when dealing with venture capitalists. You will not be able to keep your entire business to yourself in most scenarios, so you should plan to hold at least 51 percent of the business to still have the final say in all important decisions.

Besides business control, there is another important element that will strike at your ownership, and that is the lack of personal privacy regarding your business. There will be a loss of autonomy. When you borrow money from a source, often they will want to become somewhat of a partner and have a say in the decisions being made. Suddenly you have a head looking over your shoulder, asking why you are doing this and why you spent money on that. You are not as free to take chances with your business because now you have somebody who is monitoring everything that you do and expecting an explanation for each step that is being made. This can not only be costly in your own personal time, but also in the time that it will take a business to get off the ground because you will have someone investigating your progress each step of the way and hindering some of those quick decisions that need to be made. If nothing else, you may hear an earful on your every decision.

Create an agreement

Any time that you create a deal that uses OPM, always be sure to have a clear and professional contract that outlines its conditions. This is one cost that you do not want to skimp on and then learn about the hard way. If you are putting a deal together the correct way, which should involve the help and advice from a lawyer, a contract should already be a part of the package. But even so, it pays to mention from the onset the importance of having all expectations and requirements of both parties outlined. In the unfortunate case that you would ever find yourself in court because of an OPM deal that went sour, a well-written contract that you adhered to can be your best backup and defense. A lawyer can be your greatest ally whenever you are dealing with contracts and agreements. They can prove invaluable by helping to set up the agreement terms, greatly reducing the chances for future occasions of "confusion," and other issues that can arise should things not work out according to expectations.

A solid agreement will spell out those expectations of all parties involved. As an entrepreneur, you have expectations for what you expect out of the deal. State them clearly. If you believe in your business idea strongly enough to put all of your hopes and efforts into it, then you have every right to have expectations in return. Just as important, you need to be clear on the expectations of your OPM source, even if it is a family member or friend who ultimately provides you the funds. A good agreement will cover not only the financial aspects, but the communication aspects of the relationship as well. Some issues to clarify may include:

- Does your OPM source expect weekly phone calls to cover progress?

- Do they expect to receive monthly reports or statements?

- Is their only expectation that you make your loan payments on time, and they do not see a need for you to check in with them?

> **$ Investors' Insight:**
> An agreement can clarify all aspects of the relationship from the very beginning so there are no problems caused by misunderstandings as the business relationship progresses, which could lead to loopholes in the contract. A carefully crafted agreement helps ensure your rights if disagreement places you in a legal corner without protection.

Another agreement loophole that is worth mentioning is who has legal ownership of a business's liability, even when you have sold it to another party. Most OPM entrepreneurs find themselves involved with many different businesses. They cannot keep them all, nor would they maybe want to, considering that it would be a lot to keep track of and quite the time-consuming undertaking to build each one into bigger and more profitable enterprises. The problem is no matter how you word your contract of sale, there is a chance that if a problem ever occurs with the business or product you created, you could be held partially liable in a court of law for payment to those who are filing the suit. This is a little-known sales-agreement loophole that has bitten a few people over the years, so it is worth your attention to visit a business broker or insurance agent to see if this kind of coverage is a necessary precaution you should be taking to preclude it from happening on your deal.

Securities Laws

Securities laws can cause serious trouble for someone who is unaware of what these regulations are. First, let us start out by introducing securities laws as being a part of the many deals that you will be funding using OPM, which have to be taken into account before you do anything. Securities laws protect investors from potential fraud, deceit, and misrepresentations in business dealings. A lot of these business arrangements are working with an intangible investment, such as stocks or an ownership stake in a company. The idea is that you are offering a promise of a return on monies given to you by an outside source that does not fall under traditional loan setups. If the arrangement does not involve a product or tangible worth that you can wrap your hands around, chances are that it is considered to be a security, and it would be wise to pay strict attention to the following few words of warning.

The federal law has several restrictions in the case of a sale of a security. The first has to do with full disclosure. The seller of the security is required to fully disclose all material facts of the business deal, including numbers, ideas, plans, other contributors, and materials going into the project. Essentially, everything that an investor could use to make an informed decision about giving money to your idea should be included within these materials. Beyond these materials, you are also going to need to register with the Security Exchange Commission (SEC) and appropriate state agency, and you will need to publicly disclose information regarding your business operations, management, and financial state. You provide the investor with a prospectus, which must be filed with the SEC before the security is offered for sale. The SEC has to approve the registration statement before you can proceed with the sale; this process is sometimes known as "going public." It is very expensive to go public, as well as time-consuming. The business is then responsible for a variety of report disclosures and internal audits and controls, which significantly add to the cost of doing business altogether.

The SEC will be your first obstacle, but you must keep in mind that their job is to ensure that public investors are seeing the whole picture before deciding to hand over their money. They are not necessarily telling investors whether it is a sound deal or not, but under a state "blue sky" law, they will be. The blue sky laws vary from state to state, but basically consist of a review of your business standings; through the information you present, they make a decision as to whether or not your public offerings are sound.

With all of these headaches, would it not just be easier to sell these securities under the table and avoid the substantial cost and time? Of course, but that would be risky business and not advisable to look for a shortcut. If you are caught, you will most certainly be liable for not only huge penalties and fines, but in some cases, also a jail stay. A business owner who does not comply with securities laws is liable for returning the investors' money, whether the business venture succeeds or fails. In other words, investors can cash out at any time for any reason from the business and be within their right to expect full payback on demand. Too many of these and cash flow can drop severely for the business that is already struggling with the previously mentioned fines.

Exceptions to the securities laws

You undoubtedly want to know if you can find an exception from this complicated maze of laws and requirements, and there is a good possibility that one is available. Before going any further in discussing this, remember the complex nature of securities laws. Therefore, to really create a solid plan on how to deal with the registration requirements of securities laws, you must obtain legal advice from a qualified securities lawyer. Only they will be able to guide you through the pitfalls of raising funds that potentially invoke the securities laws. This section is merely meant to give you a grasp of what they are and how they may apply to your search for an OPM source, and what you may have to deal with as part of the OPM use. You need to understand the importance of following through with your fund acquisition the right way and not back yourself into any financial corners because you were not aware they existed.

The nature of whether you can obtain exception to the securities laws is dependent on the amount of money you are seeking, what you are asking from those who you are seeking it from, and the manner in which you seek the money. It should be plain to see at this point that the best way to deal with this obstacle is before you have even designed your business plan or model. Depending on the choices that you make here, you can easily avoid cost and headache. So please seek out professional advice before you put any plan into effect. Unless you are a qualified lawyer in these matters, you are already betting against your survival if you do not know what you are getting into from the beginning. Keep in mind the old legal maxim, "Ignorance of the law is no excuse." Get the qualified, expert advice you need to traverse these tricky areas of the business world, especially with securities laws. You have to make sure you are complying with the federal law, as well as your state laws.

CASE STUDY: SIMPLY NECESSARY, INC.

Simply Necessary, Inc.
7206 Hileman Drive West
Lakeland, FL 33810-4704
Phone: (863) 859-2650
Tangela@simplynecessary.com
www.simplynecessary.com
Tangela Walker-Craft — President and Owner

I acquired a bachelor's degree in English with an emphasis on creative writing from the University of South Florida. I founded Simply Necessary, Inc., in order to market and distribute a child-care product that I invented.

When I decided to go into business, I did not have to wait very long to get my business up and running. My mother immediately volunteered to invest in my idea. With funds from her savings, I combined some of the savings that my husband and I shared, and Simply Necessary was launched. If it were not for this source of OPM, I do not think I would have been able to start my company — or I would have ended up having to take out a loan.

Just because I was borrowing from a family member does not mean I did not worry about paying it back. I still fear not being able to repay my mother for her investment. Our product is well-reviewed, but a slight fear still lingers.

My biggest recommendation is to not borrow money that someone else needs, because there are no guarantees. When you do obtain OPM, I advise that you treat that money as if it were your own. Do not make rash decisions with the money.

Working with my mother in using OPM really reinforced my belief that she trusts me and has faith in my ideas. And when it comes to those funds, I believe in being very forthcoming. I think you should constantly update investors on any progress, or lack of progress.

If you are looking for OPM, be prepared to feel an overwhelming need to succeed in order to make the investor feel that they made the right decision. I was lucky, in that my pitch for OPM was not hard to make. However, knowing that someone else who had been successful believed in my idea made my mother more secure in her decision to make the investment.

Chapter 5:

Choosing a Business Entity

What to Consider in Making Your Decision

Now it is time to work on planning and strategizing, and this chapter will discuss the types of business models you can select from when you decide how to build your business and what structure it should take. And, as has become a familiar theme, each one has benefits and weaknesses to consider. There are multiple options, from the basic sole proprietorship to the more complex structure of a corporation. These represent the legal status of your business and will regulate exactly how the government will set up your taxes, as well as how efficiently your business system is going to be able to operate. How to structure your business should be a lot clearer and easy to understand in comparison to the securities laws. To help your thought process, the following provides a description of each of these business models. Because each type of structure has specific tax implications, it is recommended that you talk with an accountant and seek legal counsel to help you decide which structure is the best for you and your business.

Sole Proprietor

The sole proprietorship is essentially a business owned and operated by just one person who has claimed responsibility for all income and profits of the business, and this also unfortunately includes all of the debt. This legal form of business is considered to be the simplest structure to set up, requiring the entrepreneur only to obtain all necessary licenses, certifications, and tax identification numbers prior to the start of the new business. This legal form also involves the least government interference, which is another reason why it is the most popular form of business formed in the United States each year.

The entrepreneur who has developed a business plan that contains minimal personal liability threats would benefit most from this set-up. If you have a business with significant liability, such as a construction company, you may want to think twice about this structure for the business. In the case of an unfortunate event causing the business debts to exceed its assets, your creditors can claim your own personal assets, including your house, car, savings, and general investments.

All of this simplicity and ease of set-up also has disadvantages beyond placing your personal assets on the line. Finding quality employees who will be willing to grow with the company can prove to be quite difficult to attract, as the small-business sole proprietor has limited resources that will enable them to offer employees any immediate real benefit and future advancement. For this reason, most sole proprietors end up becoming jacks-of-all-trades and running their business by themselves, for the most part. They may have the occasional employee, but these will come and go on a rolling basis, and limit the business in its ability and potential for any serious growth.

Advantages of a Sole Proprietorship	Disadvantages of a Sole Proprietorship
They are incredibly simple and quick to set up. Owner keeps all of the profits. All income is taxed on a personal level. Business can be dissolved just as easily as it was established. One person makes all the decisions, leaving no possibility for disagreement.	The business is completely dependent on the owner. They can be hard to sell because it is dependent on the owner. Finding employees to grow the business is very challenging. Owner will have a difficult time obtaining significant capital. The owner assumes liability using his or her own personal assets.

Partnership

A partnership involves two parties who have agreed to share profits in a business venture. This legal business entity is quite similar to the sole proprietorship in many ways, with the addition of another partner assuming the right to a share of the business profit as well as the debt. However, the partnership is not always a 50/50 split, and it will be up to the two parties to decide exactly what kind of actual split of the profits and losses will be given to each partner. This can be both a benefit and a disadvantage, as a partner who assumes 70 percent of a company will receive a huge chunk of the profits, but in the event of a bankruptcy, they will unfortunately share the brunt of the loss.

This set-up may be of benefit over the sole proprietorship option because you are combining talents and splitting responsibilities, as well as combining financial resources for greater growth potential. The partnership is also traditionally just as quick and simple to set up and break down, as long as things are kept simplistic. The possibility of finding quality employees is slightly greater with a partnership than a sole proprietorship because the employees can be made aware that the potential exists of their becoming a partner at some point in the future as the business grows.

On the negative side of a partnership are the written-agreement loopholes. Unlike the sole proprietor who assumes all of the profit and risk, the partners must clearly decide how much each partner has invested in the business, the rights and responsibilities of each, how the profits will be distributed, and how the business will be split in the case of selling, adding, or subtracting partners. The biggest reason that a clear, written agreement needs to be worked out is because it is human nature to exchange the original agreed-upon plan and subjectively choose one that offers an advantage over the original, especially if the parties involved are relying on memory for the details.

However, the ultimate negative aspect of a partnership is the shared liability between partners. This means that anything one partner does can substantially affect the other partner, including any surmounting debt they may collect over the course of their partnership. This is one of the biggest reasons why partnerships are generally frowned upon these days, besides the necessity of filing separate tax returns — and the heated legal and personal disputes that can arise.

Advantages of a Partnership	Disadvantages of a Partnership
Partners share debt.	Profit sharing.
Simple and easy to set up.	Disagreements on business practices.
Each partner can take on a specialty and increase efficiency of business.	Partners are responsible for each other's debt.
Investment capital enjoys the benefit of two investors as opposed to one.	Complex written agreement in comparison to sole proprietor.
Quality employees are easier to come by with the possibility of becoming a partner in the future.	Business cannot be broken down as easily (one partner wants to sell, the other wants to expand).

There are a couple of varieties of partnership that you should be aware of, as well. These are the limited partnership (LP) and the limited liability partnership (LLP).

Limited partnership

With this form of business entity, you have at least one general partner who makes the decisions and runs the operation, and the other passive partners who do not. These passive partners are considered limited partners, and their liability in the business is also limited. However, the general partners retain full liability with their personal assets on the line.

Limited liability partnership

This is a general partnership that separates, and therefore protects, you from others in the partnership. Your only liability comes from your own actions and not from those of your partners. But even this is limited in overall liability, as the partners are still subject to the securities laws, the regular business debt, and other laws that govern regular business dealings.

Corporation

A corporation is generally thought of as being a better deal than a partnership because each partner is placed in a separate entity apart from the other owner and no longer has to worry about taking the responsibility of each other's debt. This also extends to the personal debt of the business. This means that in the case of bankruptcy or an unfavorable legal decision, the debts of the business cannot be paid to the creditors through the use of the entrepreneurs' personal assets. Each corporate partner's home, car, and savings are better protected. The corporation also has the ability to sell shares of stock ownership in the company in order to raise capital. This translates to a greater growth potential than the other two legal business entities we have discussed so far.

Another distinctive advantage over the partnership is the ability to quickly and easily change hands to other owners through the use of stock. The business is also much less dependent on the original owners, which means that this type of business has the potential to continue on and be passed from generation to generation of future partners. Employees are much more drawn to this type of legal business, being larger and having more potential for advancement and a perceived greater potential for security. The increased ability to raise capital also ensures a paycheck every month, as compared to the smaller sole proprietors and partnerships that can be vastly affected by dips in the business cycle and be forced to lay off employees during the slow times.

With these advantages, however, there must come a few disadvantages, as well as complexity. The greatest disadvantage to some is the increased taxation, which surmounts to about double the taxation of a sole proprietor or partnership. The corporation is responsible not only for paying taxes on the corporation itself, but also on the individual. On top of this tax, the corporation must additionally take into account an annual tax on all stock shares. Just the formation alone of a corporation can be costly for a small business owner due to the necessity of legal services, state fees, record book, stock certificate purchases, and quarterly state and federal reports. But, if you think you are going to do a public offering of stock in your company, you will need to be incorporated.

Of course, for the small business interested in becoming a corporation, part of these taxes can be eliminated — namely the double taxation on income — if they choose to become an S corporation, a subset of a corporation that offers a different tax arrangement. An S corporation can be taxed based on the set up of the legal partnership. To receive this privilege, however, a business must limit itself on the number and type of shareholders it can have. It can only provide so much issued stock and general sources of revenue. In other words, the corporation's ability to grow is stunted in exchange for a dramatic decrease in taxation. Depending on your expectations for your corporation's growth potential, this can be seen as either a good or bad thing. Your legal advisor should be able to decipher the best arrangement for you, dependent on your business plan and profit/loss margin.

Advantages of a Corporation	Disadvantages of a Corporation
Owners and stockholders are not liable for corporate debt. S corporations can enjoy benefits without increased taxation. Has the most potential for capital of all legal business entities. Easier time finding and keeping quality employees and specialists. Can run without owner involvement, making it more transferable.	High initial cost and complexity. Must pay an annual tax on stock shares. Double-taxed, which translates to less income. Involves the most government interference and regulation. Easy to lose control of a company if owners' stock shares fall below 50 percent.

Limited liability corporation

This type of corporation can be run by another corporation or company or by one person. You can distribute profits and losses any way you want to. A document called the Articles of Organization is filed, and the members of the corporation have an operating agreement. With an LLC, all members have limited liability. Also, there are no limits to the type or number of shareholders. This has become a very popular form of business entity for many small businesses.

For all of the entities discussed, you will want to talk with qualified tax, financial, and legal advisors, to make sure you are adhering to the laws of your state and that your particular business is setting up under the entity that will offer you the maximum benefit for your goals.

$$ Investors' Insight:

Before setting up your business entity, sketch out a plan for various contingencies should your original ideas as to how you will fund your venture do not go accordingly. This is especially helpful if you are sitting on the fence, trying to decide between two business structures. Talk with your legal and tax advisors.

Warning: A Word for the Home Business Owner

Working out of a home-office environment can be rather challenging. Not only do you have to deal with opinions from your postal carrier, clients, friends, and neighbors that you are not a "real" business; you also have to deal with the home environment, which can be laden with distraction. In fact, the biggest challenges you will face on a daily basis are not the balancing of spending charts, coordinating schedules, or executing conference calls, but instead keeping one area in your home a place for work and not allowing other distractions to take away from your professionalism. There are some measures you can take to help you, though. More than ever, it is actually quite easy to pretend you are a big corporation. All you need is an impressive Web site presence and a professional system of receiving and taking calls. You would be surprised at the number of hugely successful businesses that got started out of a basement or garage and grew into a professional office before anyone ever suspected it had been any other way.

The National Association for the Self-Employed (NASE) has a great online database that can help with advice on tax deductions, affordable health insurance, methods of screening and hiring new employees, and the latest business trends at **www.**

nase.org. Small Office Home Office (SOHO) is another helpful resource for the home business owner. It offers a wealth of advice on marketing, financing, debt, credit cards, and how to create a business plan for each step of your businesses growth at **www.soho.org**.

With the basic necessities of a successful home business met, another danger of working out of your home is finding a beginning and ending to your day. It is far too easy to continue working when you are already at home and neglect the other things in your life that are important, such as your friends and family. To gain insight into how to accomplish a smooth-running home business, Home Office Blues (**www.HomeOfficeBlues.com)** allows the start-up entrepreneur to speak to others who have been on the same entrepreneurial path and who can now offer advice and support for everything from software, hardware, clients, and even family. This is a great way to virtually get away from your office and take a break around that "virtual" water cooler.

Of course, whenever possible, you should get away from the office and be around people, listen to current events, and forget about work and home for a while. Many successful home business owners spend the first part of their morning at a coffee shop or library, interacting with others who are also in the process of starting their day. If you are not careful, your home will become a prison, a place of loneliness and banishment from the rest of the world. You may not need the use of your home to double as your business address forever — especially as it grows — but it pays to make your stay as nice as possible while it does.

CASE STUDY: INFUSIONSOFT

Infusionsoft
2065 W. Obispo Ave., Suite 103
Gilbert, AZ 85233
Phone: (866) 800-0004
www.infusionsoft.com
Clate Mask — Co-founder and CEO

I learned about OPM when I was in college, but it was not until our third year of running Infusionsoft that I realized how much I needed it to create the company I envisioned.

At first, I was hesitant to use OPM. Looking back, it was probably about two years from the time I realized I should do it to the time I was totally comfortable doing it. When I began the process, I feared that I would lose their money — and I still fear that. I think a good steward of invested funds will always be concerned about the potential loss, but that concern must be superseded by a desire to multiply the investor's money.

I would advise an entrepreneur who would like to use OPM to not take it lightly. Treat the money like your own. Once you have enough belief in your ability to multiply the investor's money, take the money and watch your business grow fast. For me, OPM helped me build a multimillion-dollar software company that will one day become a billion-dollar software company.

I found my sources of OPM first through banks, then friends, then angels, and then venture capitalists. We were always careful to use only the amount of OPM that would help us achieve the next level of success. If you use more OPM than you need, that can be a bad thing because you give up too much of the company, and you might make dumb decisions because you feel like you have a ton of money.

An entrepreneur should view the use of OPM as a way to open the opportunity to grow fast. But you also have to realize you are giving up some control by using OPM. Ultimately, you have to decide if the growth opportunity is worth using OPM, and if it is, choose your investor wisely and then go for it.

For the investors who worked with me, what they got out of the deal has varied by investor type. The banks just got a certain interest rate for their return on investment. Friends and family got a low price on the stock. Angels came on board and paid a little higher price for the stock. Venture capitalists followed the angels and paid a slightly higher price. But in the final analysis, all the investors got in at a low share price, and they will all make a big return on their investment.

If you want happy investors, then be sure to choose investors you trust, who can work with through thick and thin. Understand what their expected rate of return is and in what time frame they expect to get it. Communicate often and openly.

CASE STUDY: INFUSIONSOFT

A new entrepreneur should expect an investor to want an exit strategy and a multiple return on their money. They trust you to run the business, but you need to realize they are primarily in the game to get a healthy return on their investment in a reasonable period of time.

When we went to our OPM sources to sell them on our idea, our strengths were having a vision of where we were going, a track record of results that would lead to a reasonable belief we could accomplish the vision, and a management team they could believe in.

Chapter 6:

Planning and Preparation

What Investors Look For: Return On Investment

Once the decision is made as to the structure of your business and you get things set up, you will next be preparing to work with investors.

The first factor that must be addressed is to know exactly whom you are dealing with when you start working with them. Usually, it is very powerful people who have either inherited their money or built up an empire through aggressive dealing and risky ventures. Powerful people have learned that it takes even more money to continue to create wealth. This is the unique phenomenon we touched on before where it will be easier to interest an investor in a $100,000 venture than it is in a $10,000 one. The bigger investment is a better risk for them, as it has the possibility of gaining a substantial amount of money that brings them the type of returns they are interested in gaining.

As any gambler who is serious about hitting it big in Las Vegas knows, you are not going to hit the jackpot unless you put out an equivalent amount of big money. When was the last time you heard of someone winning big on one of the nickel machines at Treasure Island? While it could happen, the big winners are generally the ones taking the big risks. Their equivalents in the business world are the angel investors. Do not inflate your initial investment, but do reach big when you begin the planning of your business. Have the confidence to think and dream big when you are putting together your business plan and proposal. You will have an easier time finding investors interested in your project if it is on a larger scale. But you must also have the assurance, knowledge, and attitude to sell yourself to the investors and win over their confidence. This comes from doing your due diligence to support your dreams logically and with the numbers.

Understanding the Investor and Their Needs

As in any relationship, there are needs that must be met to foster a successful partnership with your investor.

Co-investors

The relationship with co-investors is the cornerstone for the success of your business. One of the most powerful steps a business owner can take is to ask his or her investors a series of questions unrelated to business. Questions should be asked after you have gained their respect about your ideas and are in the process of building a relationship. As strange as this may sound, it works. A few examples of questions to ask are:

- What was your first job?

- Who encouraged you the most when you were growing up?

- Who was your favorite teacher and why?

- How did you get started in your business?

Co-investors appreciate and respect the entrepreneur much more when they take the time to learn about them as individuals. Send thank you notes, birthday cards, holiday acknowledgements, and other thoughtful gifts.

> **$ Investors' Insight:**
> There is a saying that we have two ears and one mouth, so use them in that ratio. You may be up to your eyeballs in business planning, but take the time to listen to the people from whom you are trying to secure investment money. You will learn more that way, giving you invaluable insight into what investors want.

Bankers

When dealing with bankers, remember that many times they are simply frustrated investors themselves who do not have the money to live out their own dreams. The game plan here is to present your business plan in the hopes of getting them caught up in the excitement of your business plan. Sometimes a banker believes that they can live vicariously through such a loan and will qualify something that they may not have qualified under different circumstances. This can be a phenomenon with any investor, but it appears to be especially prominent with bankers in smaller, local branches. You have to remember that in a solid business deal, you are not only looking to have your own needs met, but you must also discover how you can meet the needs of your investor so that they will be more likely to jump with you when the time comes. People will get inspired if you are excited by your own idea.

Setting the Stage for Success

Qualify your business idea

Gary Patterson of FiscalDoctor offers a patented five-point system he uses to guide clients through the process of quantifying their ideas and making sure that they present themselves as being deserving of OPM. Receiving OPM is only half the battle because once the money is in their hands, it will be their responsibility to use it effectively. This is why Patterson also recommends discussing these steps on a semiannual basis to ensure the money continues to be used wisely. *See his Case Study at the end of this chapter.*

Source groups

There are groups in most cities that make great allies in helping an early-stage company. These people volunteer their time to answer questions and guide the new entrepreneur along the right path as they try to locate and secure OPM sources. The mistakes avoided from talking to other local people who have been in your same situation could save you thousands, if not millions, of dollars.

Education

To be successful in business, surround yourself with people who have been successful in business. Education is a top priority and should be on-going. Use a variety of educational means to learn all you can as you work to reach your goals, such as lectures, group meetings, classes, coaching sessions, and anything else that offers time with experts who use OPM. Spending money on education and coaching is money well-spent.

There are also a number of additional resources that can be used beyond this one to further your understanding of the art of OPM. These sources are listed at the back of this book. There is no end to the creative number of ways of achieving OPM, and the best way to decide on your own technique is to do as much research as you can and then incorporate the ideas into your business plan. *This subject will be elaborated on more in Chapter 7.* The purpose of this book is to combine a number of expert techniques, opinions, and advice to give you a clear idea of the different forms of OPM from which professionals are currently profiting. Also, just as markets and economics change, so too will the ways in which you will be securing OPM.

Research

Although education will be an ongoing endeavor in your professional life, you will need to do some more pointed research specific to getting your business idea launched. Investors will want to see that you have done your homework, that you know what you are getting into, and that you have a plan to succeed.

Your ultimate goal will be in the hard-copy format of the business plan, which you can think of as the Bible of any business enterprise. It will be used to sway investors to commit to your endeavors. You will also use it as a navigational tool and manual to guide you through operating your business, as it will be the repository for all of the goals, facts, and figures needed to succeed.

To begin your research, go to your local county library and visit the business resources section. This may be located at the larger library branches in your county. In this section, you will find the resources you will need to hone in on the fine details that will make up your business plan.

The Internet provides a wide range of information as well and can be used to figure out the details needed for your specific goals, locate information on your competitors, and discover what the outlook is for your industry.

Teasing Out the Details

When you are preparing your research, there are some overall goals to keep in mind to save time and effort. You are looking to fill in the blanks that cover how to make your business successful, such as how the market looks for your enterprise, how much it will cost you to get operational, how much money you will need to stay operational, and how you will grow your enterprise.

Your business plan will give solid details on all of these aspects. To begin with, take your idea and figure out how to classify it. There is a system to classify industries called the North American Industry Classification System codes (NAICS), formerly the Standard Industrial Classification, or SIC, codes. Some resources still use the SIC codes, but the NAICS is the most current classification system.

To locate the code for your industry, you can go to NAICS Association (**www.naics.com**), an organization that provides free access of those codes. You will need this code when trying to dig into the more minute details regarding your particular industry. If you need to find the comparable SIC code, you can also find it through the association's site.

Another excellent resource is the U.S. Census Bureau (**www.census.gov**), which will provide economic census data. Your NAICS code will be useful here to get your industry's specifics. If you are offering a product or service, you will want to learn about the demographics for your area, as these will be your prospects and customers. Your library may keep a current book in the reference section called the Sourcebook of ZIP Code Demographics, which will provide you with a breakdown to the ZIP codes for all of the United States.

At some point, you will have to stop researching and start putting all of that information you have amassed into a beneficial, workable document. The information you have will be used to answer the many questions an investor may have regarding your business. The more solid your data, and the fact that you took the time to do the detailed research to find it, will help an investor feel more comfortable about placing his or her money in your enterprise. They want to know that you are worth the risk and that on the other side of their investment, there is great potential for a healthy return on their investment.

The next section covers the actual business plan and provides you with a working format to pull it together. It will also give you specifics on ways to use your research material to best answer the questions regarding your business. It will also show you how some of those resources fit with particular areas of your business plan. This next section can be used as a roadmap to guide your research so that you will have an idea of what you are actually looking for.

CASE STUDY: FISCALDOCTOR

FiscalDoctor

www.fiscaldoctor.com

Gary Patterson, C.P.A., M.B.A. — President and CEO

I recommend looking for an entrepreneurial group that holds morning or evening sessions. The mistakes avoided from talking to other local people who have been in your same situation can save you thousands, if not millions, of dollars.

The best place to find these groups is through word-of-mouth information, such as through your lawyer or CPA. They may not always know, but most of these service professionals who help early-stage companies are involved with these networks and have attended them. Your advisory board may have suggestions on a group to attend as well. You should make sure you are with a group that is offering up-to-date information and working to invite the best talent in your area for speaking engagements.

When Patterson is helping a company develop a business model, toward the end of this process, he addresses a few questions to make sure the project they are building is on the right track. It is amazing how detailed some businesses get into the initial planning process, but once the basic plan is in effect, they forget to continue to plan. Nothing goes along as planned; it is the way it is, and to make the best use out of the money you have worked so hard for, you should make sure at least on a quarterly basis for the first year that everything is on track, everybody is on the same page, and there is no question in anyone's mind as to what the goal is. Here are the questions Patterson uses for such a purpose:

What are the three best opportunities we could create longer term and what do we need to do to best pursue those opportunities?

Patterson suggests three to five years in the future for the business. If this question is asked and an important opportunity has been left out, the question must then be asked, "Why was that idea not included?" Depending on the answer to that question, it should raise strategic issues that should be thought about and added in the future.

What are the top three concerns you have about meeting this year's budget?

It is easier to admit to a problem and address it, than to ignore it and suffer the consequence later. Sometimes it may seem easiest to place your head in the sand and hope that everything is going to turn out. Perhaps there were a few things that cost more money than first thought, or maybe you are behind schedule from your original product release date. Patterson recommends gauging the

CASE STUDY: FISCALDOCTOR

importance of an issue by how many members of your board have mentioned the same concern. These concerns need to be addressed openly and honestly, which leads to the next question.

What actions can we take to minimize the risk of those concerns for this year's budget?

There was a time when this would have been called contingency planning. Contingency planning is defined as a business plan that confronts the likelihood of any disaster, no matter how rare, which prepares them to be able to continue without interruption or loss of control. It is never too soon to begin planning for the worst. This is as important as the initial plan for the best that landed you the OPM in the first place. Following these short-term thoughts, the venturing group must then look at these possibilities from the vantage point of three to five years into the future.

What are the three top longer-term risk area concerns of the company today, and how would the company react if those concerns materialized?

Thinking long-term, within three to five years, the key parties of the business venture must ask themselves what the risk areas are for things that could come not only now, but in the future, and decide how they would need to deal with them. Patterson admits people will tell you it is impossible to anticipate everything that could happen; this is coined by the common phrase "analysis by paralysis." Patterson, however, rebuts such thinking and reminds us that if you prioritize what you consider the top issues and plan, then when a problem does occur, the group has developed information that will help organize how the problem should be dealt with and who will be responsible for what. The problem can then be handled more quickly than if it had come about without prior strategic planning.

What are the three most crucial infrastructure issues we face over the next one or two years?

The final question is more advanced thinking for the business, but it is worth the effort to answer. Such thinking should focus on things such as the experience levels of the employees that will be necessary to carry out the business plan, any potential information technology or software problems, and so forth. It is always simpler to plan for the future when you have developed an extensive model or spreadsheet that describes what the issues and deliverables are that drive the extensive plan that will need to be executed to make it happen.

Chapter 7:

The Art of the Business Plan

The Business Plan

Just as an architect works his or her magic using a visual guide, entrepreneurs work their own magic with a similar set of plans. As an entrepreneur, if you are confident in your plan and portray your confidence through the presentation of your business plan, people will feel much more confident doing business with you. Even bankers, who you may think only look at the numbers, will be more willing to take a chance with someone who can prove he or she has a great plan than with someone who is unsure or unclear about what he or she is trying to accomplish.

You need to have three vital bits of information with you when you approach a lender with your plan. You need:

- To describe your exact business idea from start to finish.

- To give an account for how the money you are asking for will be spent.

- To back up your ideas with proof of how you know it is all going to work.

As mentioned earlier in the book, to gain the attention of private source money, you have to think big, then follow through by presenting big. For example, let us say you are looking to borrow money for a restaurant. If you approach an investor for $500,000 to open one restaurant, you are going to have a more difficult time than if you ask to borrow $5 million to open a chain. The key: Once you have achieved their attention with your dream, sell it to them and prove how it will be accomplished and why you are the best person to accomplish this.

The best way to package your presentation is with a solid business plan. A business plan should ideally encompass every imaginable scenario that your business idea could fall into and how you plan on dealing with them. It is a breakdown of dollars that must be spent to make a predicted sum of money. These numbers should not just be numbers you figured out on the back of a napkin, but rather solid evidence, using current market values, sales, and professional projections of its future. It is recommended that you elicit the help of several professionals during this process. These may include a lawyer, an accountant, and various other specialists who have experience in your business venture.

What questions should the business plan address?

To enhance the investor's understanding and knowledge of the target market you are trying to reach, there are several questions that must be addressed by a good business plan:

1. First and foremost, what is the need for the product or service you are offering?

2. What is the defined market you are trying to reach?

3. Who is going to be your main competition in the market you are servicing?

4. Is your competition successful?

5. What percentage of the market share does your competition hold?

6. Is the market you are trying to enter too saturated?

7. Is it growing, stable, or volatile?

8. What are your steps to reach this market?

9. What are a few of the business models of your competition, and can they be beat?

10. What have customers from the past expected from this type of product or service?

11. How do you see this changing in the future?

12. How much are customers willing to pay for the product or service you offer?

13. What differentiates you from your competitors?

> **$ Investors' Insight:**
> The above questions will help you more accurately strategize how to make your business a viable one, or if you should reconsider your business idea altogether. You can discover potential threats and opportunities before you have ever put the first nickel into the enterprise.

The basic structure of a business plan

The basic business plan has room for creative expression, which is highly recommended. Venture investors are accustomed to seeing business plans day-in and day-out, and the ones that will stick out in their minds are the ones that show extra care, attention to detail, and creative insight into the intended market and audience. With this in mind, you are left to be inspired by your own creative impulses, but you have here the basic ingredients that every successful business plan must cover. A note about creativity: Aim to inspire your reader, not be outlandish or outrageous. You want your plan to be remembered for the *right* reasons.

Executive summary

Think of a business plan as being similar to a résumé. The cover letter is one of the most important doors, as it will pull the reader in, tell them what you have to offer, and show why they should bother turning the page and continue to read your specifics in detail. Attention spans are short, so you want to lead strong from the very beginning. The executive summary is a one-page summary of your idea, including all of the material you will be covering throughout the rest of the proposal. Bankers and venture capitalists normally do not read further than the first page, so this is your opportunity to capture their attention before your hard work is thrown away and dismissed as a weak idea. Be sure to accent the attractive elements of the plan, paying particular attention to the profits they can expect from the venture. Think and present big; show the investors the exceptional profit possibilities the venture will offer.

Company summary

The next part of the typical business plan entails a thorough description of the business you intend to create. This is the basic description that should include the address of the proposed business and legal form in which the business will be run (LLC or general partnership), and any important key figures that will be involved in the company's creation or expansion.

Service or product for sale

This is the easiest part of the business plan, where you detail exactly what service or product you will be selling. It is a good idea to discuss not only your initial line of products and services, but also to look several years into the future and how you project the line growing. In the initial business-plan meeting, the addition of prototypes for each of these products can be a huge boost of confidence for the investor. Examples will show your dedication to the idea. You do not know what will move the investor to action; some may be interested in numbers, while others may be interested in the product itself. Do not skimp on this part — make sure the investors walk away with a clear idea of what you are selling.

Market analysis

A business plan is not worth the paper it is printed on unless it can prove the ability of the business to generate sales. While the analysis can be complicated, there are simple, easy-to-follow steps for defining the problem, analyzing the business atmosphere, collecting data, interpreting the data, solving problems, and designing the plan. Let us look at these in detail:

1. **Defining the problem:** You cannot solve anything unless you are able to understand and articulate what the problem is that needs solving. It may not be a problem as much as it is an aspect of success that past companies in your market have failed to accomplish to the degree that you are determined to do.

   - What specific marketing strategies have been utilized before regarding your idea?

   - How much money has been allocated to marketing by the competition?

- What need are you filling?

- Why should customers choose you over the competition?

- How is your product different from similar products?

- What drives customers to purchase from your competitors?

- Should you enhance your current product or service to make you more competitive?

- Who are your customers going to be?

- How can you attract new customers?

- What will keep those customers coming back to you?

2. **Collecting and analyzing data:** This is an analysis of the business marketplace that helps to define the problem in detail. These important details should include information on your customers and competition. The information should be a combination of primary and secondary research. Primary research refers to information that you collect through surveys, phone interviews, and other mediums. You may choose to use this resource to collect information to answer any of the questions from step one that you were having problems answering. Your secondary resources can come from a variety of data found at your local library in their business center, or on the Internet. The Internet will be very helpful as you begin searching for information about your competition by typing their name, industry, or region into a

search engine. You can locate the Web sites of your competitors to see what they are doing in terms of reaching your market. From this research, you will be able to pull some inside information to use in your plan and support your problem-solution scenario. Other secondary resources can be found through:

- The **U.S. Department of Commerce** publishes the *U.S. Industrial Outlook* every January, which provides a general forecast of the industries in the year to come.

- The **U.S. Census Bureau** provides Consumer Information Reports (CIRS), offering inside information on inventories, consumption, and the number of competitors in each industry.

- The **NAICS and SIC Manuals** provide the codes that are used to classify all major industries. This will help you to locate very detailed industry information as compiled by government agencies. All industries are classified under a code, and you will need to know yours, as well. You will see it appear on tax forms to add to the overall compilation figures for your industry.

- The **Business Rankings Annual** provides information regarding industries, competitors, and demographics.

3. **Interpreting the data**: This is where the statistics and analysis are turned into numbers and evidence that your idea is viable and poised to create profitable results. Your numbers support your projections. For example, if you are

projecting that your business will sell 400,000 units, your evidence will be based on your buying market's demographics, the trend for demand, and why the trend will continue. If what you are offering is a new product or service, you will show the problem that you are solving — using numbers wherever possible — and how your solution to the problem will generate sales.

4. **Solving the problem**: This is where all the results of the analysis are combined and a solution to improve upon the problem that past companies have faced will be unveiled to the investor(s). It can include any necessary details to show how the numbers you crunched from Step 3 will become more favorable using your solution.

5. **Designing the plan**: The final step is to design your plan by using the problem as its driving factor. You do this by reaching above and beyond the initial problem, showing how you intend to market and sell your idea or service. You want your business plan to have a unified message that covers all bases and shows how successful your idea will be using the research you have done as backup.

Business Plan Workshop: Worksheets for Building an Attractive Business Plan

The following is a worksheet-format business plan to help guide you in your initial preparations. One thing cannot be stressed enough: It is crucial to have a solid business plan to go along with your OPM acquisition. Without a professional and thorough business plan, locating funds for any business plan will prove to be impossible at best. This is truly the time to put your best foot

forward and offer a polished, comprehensive analysis to support your endeavor.

There are several sources that can help you with the preparation of your business plan at low or no cost if you have any further questions beyond the scope of this section. These sources include:

- Local university outreach centers
- Local university development centers
- Local university extension offices
- Local state and county economic development centers
- Women's business center

Check your local white pages or government office to help you locate these services. There are programs available to assist you, so the time you spend doing the small amount of research required to find them will offer payback in terms of time, effort, and a professional business plan that will bring you the results you are working to achieve.

The following are sample worksheets that you can use to begin forming your business plan. These worksheets can serve as a guide for the research you will be doing, helping you pull together the types of details that investors will want to know.

Marketing plan

Your **marketing plan** consists of all of the potential customers who will purchase your product or service. It is a study of your target market: who is buying, why they are buying, and how you will surpass the competition and get that market to buy from you. If you are selling products, your plan would also cover how you plan to get those products to your customers, including the details of packaging and distributing them to the market.

Marketing Plan Worksheet

Who are your customers going to be?

_____

Who are your competitors?

_____

How can you compete in this market?

_____

What are your strengths and weaknesses in comparison to competitors?

_____

What can you do better than your competitors?

_____

Are there any governmental or legal factors affecting your business?

_____

What advantages does your product have over the competition?

_____

What type of image do you want for your product?

_____

What features will be emphasized?

_____

What is your pricing strategy?

_____

Is your pricing in line with your image?

_____

Do your prices properly cover costs?

_____

What types of promotion will you use? (Television, radio, direct mail, personal contacts, newspaper, magazines, Yellow Pages, billboard, Internet, classifieds, and trade associations.)

_____

Income statement

Your **income statement** is also known as a profit and loss statement (P&L). What it shows is your business's profitability — revenue from what has been sold minus costs to run the business.

Income Statement Worksheet	
Sales/revenue	[+] _____
Variable expenses	[-] _____
Fixed expenses	[-] _____
Net profit/Net loss	[=] _____
Tax owed	[- from Net] _____

Balance sheet

A **balance sheet** is used to look at the business at a given point in time, which means it is a fluid financial statement. It is what your business owns in assets and owes as liabilities. As a new venture, you may be bringing in office equipment that you already own that you are giving to the company as a start-up asset, and of course, you will have expenses as you get the business up and running.

Balance Sheet Worksheet	
Company name	_____
Assets (dollar amount)	
Current cash assets	_____
Accounts receivable	_____
Inventory	_____
Short-term investments	_____
Long-term investments	_____
Fixed (land) expenses	_____

Equipment	_____
Furniture	_____
Automobile	_____
Other	_____
Total assets:	$ _____
Liabilities (dollar amount)	
Current liabilities	_____
Accounts payable	_____
Interest	_____
Taxes payable	_____
Federal income tax	_____
State income tax	_____
Self employment tax	_____
Property tax	_____
Payroll accrual	_____
Owner equity	_____
Capital stock	_____
Retained earnings	_____
Surplus paid in	_____
Net worth	_____
Other	_____
Total liabilities:	$ _____

Cash flow statement

The **cash flow statement** shows how much cash is needed to run the business and when that cash is needed. Basically, it is the budget for your business. Not every month will look the same, because maybe you have a quarterly or annual payment that comes due in a certain month. A cash flow statement can be kept for a given time period, such as monthly, and accrued for greater time periods, such as quarterly and annually.

Source of Cash Flow

What is your source of cash? (Sales, loans, equity invested.)

_____

_____

What are your expenses to be paid?

_____

_____

What is your balance? (Monthly cash receipts minus monthly accounts payable.)

_____

_____

What are the factors that can affect your cash flow? (This includes seasonal, returns, and payment terms.)

_____

_____

Cash Flow Statement Worksheet

Company name	_____
Cash on hand	_____
Cash receipts	_____
Cash sales	_____
Cash paid out	_____
Gross wages	_____
Payroll	_____
Office supplies	_____
Maintenance	_____
Advertising	_____
Automobile	_____
Travel	_____
Accounting	_____
Legal	_____

Rent/utilities	_____
Telephone	_____
Insurance	_____
Taxes	_____
Interest	_____
Loan principle	_____
Start up cost	_____
Escrow	_____
Bad debt	_____
Miscellaneous	_____
Total cash flow:	$ _____

(Add each entry per time period, such as January, February, and so on to arrive at the total cash flow for that month.)

Income projection

An **income projection** is a forecast of the income you expect the business to earn and the expenses you expect to accrue.

Income Projection Worksheet		
Total net sales	[+]	_____
Cost of sales	[-]	_____
Gross profits	[=]	_____
Expenses	[-]	
Salaries		_____
Payroll		_____
Legal		_____
Accounting		_____
Marketing		_____
Automobile		_____

Office supplies	_____
Utilities	_____
Rent	_____
Depreciation	_____
Insurance	_____
Permits	_____
Licenses	_____
Loan payments	_____
Miscellaneous	_____
Profit loss (pre-tax)	_____
Taxes	_____
Profit loss (post-tax)	_____

Pricing strategy

A **pricing strategy** will help guide you in choosing the right prices for your product, based on your marketing research.

The above worksheets cover the financial details of your plan, and a calculator will come in handy as you work through those.

How you track your particular business is a discussion you should have with your tax advisor. Next, we will cover what to be sure to include in your business plan to make it a well-rounded document.

Pricing Strategy Worksheet

Cost per item

Materials _____

Labor _____

Other _____

Total: _____

Overhead of production

Utilities _____

Machine depreciation _____

Automobile _____

Other _____

Total: _____

Overhead of business

Advertising _____

Promotion _____

Professional Services _____

Other _____

Total: _____

Shipping/Handling

Packaging _____

Insurance _____

Postage _____

Other _____

Total: _____

Grand Total (Wholesale):_____

(Now you must either double or triple your wholesale price in order to get your retail price. This is the price you will want to market your product at so that you can cover the expense of the product and still make a profit. If you are offering a service, you will need to break down your hours into units: What is the cost per hour? This is the hourly rate you want to achieve.)

Finalize Your Plan

When you are done with your worksheets and research, you will distill all of those elements down into the final business plan. The following will help you lay out the information in a systematic way so that you have covered all the points pertaining to the business idea while making it easy for your investors to follow.

Cover sheet

This should include your company name, company logo, company trademark, name, address, other pertinent contact information of owner, and a confidentiality clause.

Table of contents

This should detail the layout of your current business plan in a page or so, listing the headings and sub-headings.

Summary

This should outline the purpose and key points of your business:

- Type of business
- Product or service
- Company goals
- Company objectives
- Business history

Mission statement

Describe the business and what your aspirations are for it. Do not forget to mention the reason for its existence.

Executive summary

This is where you give a brief overview of the business plan:

- How is the business entity set up?

- For how long has the business been operating?

- Who is your target market?

- What are the bottom-line growth projections for the next couple of years?

- What are the competitive advantages of the business? This can include the owner's experience in the particular field.

Marketing plan

The information from your worksheet and any additional information that is pertinent to your business idea should be placed in an easy-to-read order:

- Describe your products or services

- Describe the trends in your industry

- Describe your competition

- Describe how your business differs from the competition

- Describe the customers that your business will target

- Describe your market area

- Describe your target market base

Product

If you are putting something concrete into the marketplace, you will need to be able to explain to potential investors what it is, what it can do, and what will make it successful:

- What is your product going to do?

- How will you sell the product?

- How will you market the product? (Include specific advertising methods and media you plan to use, and dates for launching each one.)

- What is your pricing strategy?

Customer service

How do you plan to keep your clients and customers satisfied in doing business with you?

Operations

This is your day-to-day plan to provide customer service and operate your business:

- Where is the business located?

- Who are the key personnel and the employees? (If it is just the business owner, give an overview of the résumé, highlighting achievements and experience.)

- How will the business make money?

- How will the business conduct monetary transactions?

- What supplies are needed to efficiently and successfully run the business?

- List your supplies and suppliers.

- Do you foresee any problems with the price or demand of supplies?

- What is your organizational set up? (Provide an organizational chart.)

Information about your business

What is the legal business form, and why is it the best option for the business? (Sole proprietorship, limited liability corporation, corporation, or partnership):

- What are your business license requirements?

- What are the zoning requirements?

- Has your business complied with all building health codes? Are there any other regulations?

- List all trademarks, patents, licenses, and copyrights needed.

Exit strategy

This is where you offer your plan to cover all eventualities, including death of the business owner or dissolving of the business entity. *This will be discussed in more detail later on in this chapter.* In the business plan, it rounds out the total picture, making your wishes for the business known from beginning to end.

Financial plan

- How will you finance the business enterprise?

- How will you manage finances?

- What parts of the business need to be financed?

Cash flow

Your financial report should be broken out monthly to show incoming and outgoing cash flow. It should include:

- Cash from sales

- Start-up costs

- Operating expenses (includes payroll, debts, rent, advertising)
- Closing balance for each month

Income statement

Your monthly breakdown should show the yearly amount in sales, expenses, and net income. It should include:

- Income
- Cost of goods sold
- Gross profit
- Operating expenses
- Taxes
- Net income

The Bottom Line

You have to remember that your business plan is the ultimate key to your success. Without a thought-out and deeply researched business plan, your business could be doomed to certain failure, becoming one of those statistics on the number of start-up businesses that fail each year. It is hard enough to go into business without having done the rudimentary research, let alone the fine details that can show potential investors your likelihood of success. Therefore, it cannot be emphasized enough regarding the necessity of having a strong vision and a solid plan to prepare for that success before it can ever happen. By taking the time to go through these steps, you will be giving your business a strong chance for success.

> **$ Investors' Insight:**
> Make sure your business plan has no spelling errors. You do not want someone reading your business plan to judge you as not having great attention to detail. The details *do* matter, so make them error-free.

A business plan is not easy to pull together, and it includes elements you may not be familiar with. It is highly recommended that you visit a business plan advisor if any detailed questions come up that need specific attention. The sample worksheets are meant as a general overview and outline of the steps necessary to build upon your ideas. Every business has its own details that must be dealt with a little differently in order to operate and function successfully; this is where a personal advisor can provide details that would have been impossible to have included within the wide scope of this book.

Each business enterprise is unique, from the service or product offered, to the competitive advantage, to the background of the business owner. As such, every business plan is unique to that particular enterprise. Also, it should be viewed as a living document that will change throughout the life of the business as new situations and opportunities arise. You may use it daily to make sure your business is on the projected track and revise it as often, or it may be something you revisit quarterly and tweak. It will provide the finger on the pulse of your business when used, rather than gather dust on your bookshelf.

Business plan software programs

There are also good business-planning software programs that are designed to take you through this analysis step by step in a more guided format. Below are a couple of available software programs. You can also go online and search for "business plan software."

Business Plan Pro, by Palo Alto Software: With more than 500 sample business plans, this program will walk you step-by-step through creating a business plan. The standard edition is about $100 and is available at **www.paloalto.com/business_ plan_software.**

PlanWrite, by Business Resource Software: This program offers a variety of sample business plans along with phone support. The price starts at about $50 and is available at **www.brs-inc.com.**

Exit Strategy

You are trying to get your business up and running, and maybe the last thing you want to think about is how to end it. But as part of a complete business plan, you should include a section devoted to exactly what your plans are for the business you have built, so it is worth taking the time to understand why you should include it. Just as you plan for how your business will be launched, it is a good idea to plan for what will happen to the business should there be a death, should you wish to get out of it and start a new one, or should you be done altogether. It should be spelled out clearly so that you can use it as a goal to work toward, or so that someone following behind you will know your intent.

An exit strategy will be of special interest to your investors. They want to know what your plan is to get them a return on their investment and an idea of when you expect this to occur. The marketing and financial aspects of the business plan show the birth of your enterprise, while the exit strategy shows the long-

term goals and growth over time. It also shows potential investors that you have thought this through from inception to possible end and have planned for all contingencies. Also, similar to a beacon, a solid exit strategy can provide an excellent tool that will help guide you in your daily operations and management keeping you on course to reach your vision. The exit plan serves as the icing on the proverbial cake and makes a tidy beginning to an end scenario.

There are several options to consider including in your exit plan that will show the direction in which you envision the company going. These include:

- **Stock offering:** Offer shares in your company to the public. Stocks can be converted to cash.

- **Sell:** Sell company old to new owners but retain the identity you created.

- **Acquisition**: Build your company to a point that another company will want to purchase it.

- **Merger:** Join forces with another company.

- **Franchise:** Receive cash for the replication of your idea; you are no longer operating a business daily. The business may be one that can be duplicated elsewhere, over and over.

- **Pass on to family:** Transfer the management of your company to your children or other family members.

- **Close operations:** Cease and desist business operations altogether at some point, depending on your type of business. In effect, you are shuttering the windows and closing the door.

Also, your investors will want to know how they will recoup their investment should you pass away before your goals are fully realized — and their profits earned and paid out. Your family should be aware, too. One factor that far too many do not realize is that when they die, if they do not have a specific exit strategy for paying off their debts and leaving money for their family, they are leaving them open to disaster. The OPM debt you have created, which otherwise would be paid off as the business venture continues, would fall on the family should you die. Because most families would not have the ability to take over the business, they are forced to liquidate its assets to close any debt the business has incurred. There are many stories of millionaire entrepreneurs whose fortunes were quickly lost within a few years after they died because of poor planning. Joe Robbie, original owner of the Miami Dolphins, is one such story.

In 1990, Robbie died unexpectedly at age 73, leaving his family without an exit plan for his business entities and what would happen with them. The family was forced to auction off much of his estate. Robbie's business planning was unfortunately incomplete because he did not include what to do about estate taxes, which resulted in his family being left with a reported $47 million in estate taxes. Over the next four years, his family's net worth dissolved, leaving them with what appeared to be no other alternative than to sell the one thing of value left in their possession: the Miami Dolphins and the Joe Robbie Stadium (now Pro Player

Stadium). They sold these assets for $138 million — a fraction of the original value — in order to cover the estate taxes, in effect losing the assets and the ability to continue Robbie's intended legacy. As of 2008, the value of the Miami Dolphins is estimated at $1 billion, according to **www.Forbes.com**.

The Robbie story highlights a simple fact: This type of financial fiasco can be easily avoided with proper, thorough planning. Robbie put up private funds to launch his dream, earned it back, and created a vast estate. But that earned business money was not protected in any way, leaving it open to estate taxes. You will have to ask yourself if the risk is worth the possible outcome of leaving your family with nothing, or the liquidation of your business efforts. And is that risk worth it when there are so many other alternatives at your disposal that use OPM?

CASE STUDY: CONCEPTS IN SUCCESS

Concepts in Success
jestrin@conceptsinsuccess.com
www.conceptsinsuccess.com
Phone: (954) 727-8206
Josh Estrin — Business consultant, radio personality, and author of *Shut Up! And Listen To Yourself*

Few people can come to the table unless they come from a family with old money or have saved money their entire lives. It is not easy to have the available funds it takes to create a successful business simply out of the entrepreneur's own assets or savings. Around 90 percent of the American economy is driven by what is considered small business (fewer than 500 employees), and they likely do not have a large source of money from which they can draw whenever they need.

This means you will have to look to OPM. Larger sums of money tend to be easier to get, because savvy business people do not want to invest in something that is going to give them a $10,000 to $20,000 return. It is scary for someone to ask for $1 million, $2 million, or $10 million. When we are talking about starting a company, we are talking about some serious capital. However, the people you will be talking to are used to hearing those numbers all the time, even though you

CASE STUDY: CONCEPTS IN SUCCESS

may not be. If you were an investor and someone came to you with an idea that they needed $50,000, the one question you might say to yourself is: What the heck are they going to do with $50,000? They are going to blow through that within the first couple of months.

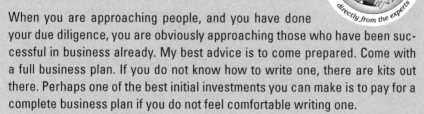

When you are approaching people, and you have done your due diligence, you are obviously approaching those who have been successful in business already. My best advice is to come prepared. Come with a full business plan. If you do not know how to write one, there are kits out there. Perhaps one of the best initial investments you can make is to pay for a complete business plan if you do not feel comfortable writing one.

Keep in mind that these are people who want measurable outcomes. They do not want to invest in something that you know will work, just because you said so. Come to the table with a market analysis, a prototype (if it is a product), a one- to seven-year plan, a list of potential market niches and clients, and a strategic plan. The more information you can show people to prove to them that you are going to succeed, the better chance you have of their taking a calculated risk.

Also, you really need to connect yourself with a mentor. You cannot be an expert on everything. It is really great to pick up the phone and ask someone, "Is this a direction I should be going in?" Of course, I go with what I think is best, butsurrounding myself with information is equally — if not more than — powerful to the actual resource of dollars and cents.

When it comes to going to family as a source of OPM, you can ask any expert: Whether it is your wife, your sister, your father, or Aunt Phyllis, it is always best to keep this as a business agreement.

Another avenue to look at from all sides are angel investors and venture capitalists. The line between an angel investor, which can be a very misleading term, and a venture capitalist has blurred. Angel investors used to be much kinder in the way that they gave you your money; they were not as tactical as they are today. Now what we have are individual angel investors forming angel groups.

I have had experience with an angel benefactor. I had someone who had the means to help me start a business and, because they found what I did interesting, they could live vicariously through what I was doing. It was all written out on paper, but there was never any expectation to pay the money back. This benefactor was a creative individual who was also an accomplished corporate attorney. He was stuck writing contracts and negotiating business deals all day. I came along with public relations and marketing experience, a book, a radio show, and a con-

CASE STUDY: CONCEPTS IN SUCCESS

nection to the pop-culture world, and he now had the ability to write entertainment contracts, negotiate appearances, and go to red carpet events. He was paid back with the opportunity to be involved with a world that intrigued him.

When you are dealing with OPM, part of the deal can be exactly what I have talked about. Maybe the full amount is not paid back, but the expectation, depending on the company, to go to trade shows, high-end events, or connections is worth the money. This is unique and depends on what kind of company you are starting. Most people start a company that sells a product, service, or both. You are usually looking at people starting companies that make software, T-shirts, clothing, or fragrances. These are companies that an investor may find interesting because they will be able to go to fashion shows or other events. Maybe fashion is something that has always interested them, but they just never had an entrance. This can be a negotiating point with some people.

As for using OPM from venture capitalists, you need to be very careful because without knowing it, you can end up having to turn your company over to the investors. The venture capitalist is not out to take an adventure, but to increase his or her personal capital by investing in your venture. I have known a lot of people who have turned around and created extremely successful businesses, and realized that 51 percent of the company is owned by someone else.

Success begets success. OPM is a way to not only start a business, but a way to take it from its initial launching to the next level. If a business cannot grow and sustain itself, then you need to be very careful, because if you infuse $1 million into a business that does not already have the infrastructure to support it, then the money is going to go into the toilet.

All businesses go through cycles, and oftentimes a business that has been around three to five years is poised to take itself to the next level, but it does not have the working capital to do that. That is when businesses go to banks and ask for lines of credit, and go to the investors and ask for money. You need to show them what strategically you are going to do with their money. For example, say your company is now grossing $2 million and should really be grossing $10 million or $20 million. If they are willing to give you $5 million, you know you can do it.

Chapter 8:

Financing Options

Conventional OPM Resources in Debt Financing

Credit cards

Credit cards are one of the easiest loans given to people today, but they can also be one of the most dangerous. For the person receiving a credit card, they seemingly have the most to gain, as this loan is generally unsecured: The lender is taking on the full risk that if you do not pay back the loan, they cannot legally take anything from you without a complex legal battle. This does not mean that they cannot make borrowers' lives a living nightmare and ruin their credit for the next seven years, which is how long bad debt will continue to be reported and appear on your credit report.

Seven years might seem bearable, but this is where borrowers have the most to lose: Credit cards can really get you on their fees and ultra-high interest rates. Using enough borrowed credit, entrepreneurs could soon find themselves paying three times the original amount in interest or late fees if they are not careful, which is an absolute waste of resources that could be used to grow the business. Before laying a heaping amount of borrowed cash on the line via a credit card, make sure that you have a thorough plan for payback so you are not saddled with those interest fees for a long period of time. Calculate how much this short-term loan will "cost" in terms of the interest fees. Then weigh the advantages against the disadvantages:

Advantages	Disadvantages
You are almost guaranteed the loan up to the maximum of your total credit availability. You will not have to fill out a lengthy application or have a waiting period that would hold up receipt of the money. You will not have to go through a credit-score process when you want the cash. You can pay back the loan immediately, or take as long as needed, just honoring the minimum balance due.	You may eventually fill your card to the limit, rendering it useless during times you may really need it, such as those unexpected emergencies. Credit card debt can become incredibly expensive if you are only paying the minimum balance, which may mostly be interest rather than the principal amount. A variable interest rate can cause the interest fees to trend upward, costing you even more than you may have allotted for.

Collateral loans

On the other end of the spectrum from the use of credit cards for access to capital, you will find a secured type of loan. The advantage here will be a decreased interest rate due to less risk that the lender has to take on, but at the same time, an increased risk for the borrower, because something of theirs is being used for collateral. Such collateral could be stocks, bonds, land, a house, or a condominium. But collateral loans can be a detriment to you in the event of a default. This is when you may be faced with the possibility of the collateral's — your house or car that you have put up — being sold in order to pay off your debt. A double whammy can occur if the item you were using for collateral does not sell for as much as they thought it would; then you will still owe additional cash on the loan along with losing your personal assets. This is the reason why most experts will recommend borrowing several thousand dollars fewer than your total collateral, just in case of such an unforeseen circumstance. In general, however, with most sources of traditional loans you will only want to borrow what you need. The only time when borrowing more than what you need could be a cushion is when you are using OPM, as there will not be an overly large interest rate compared to credit cards or collateral loans for you to drown in.

Advantages	Disadvantages
Ability to secure a decreased interest rate for the loan in comparison to an unsecured loan. Generally, collateral loans are a fairly simple and guaranteed method for receiving funds.	Your personal assets are put up to cover the risk of the loan. If your loan defaults and the collateral does not cover the total loan amount, the entrepreneur is still responsible for the remaining debt.

Lease financing

Lease financing is not necessarily a means for cash as much as it is an alternative to acquire necessary supplies or equipment for your business. This financing is available through finance companies, banks, and sometimes even the firms that sell the equipment. The leaser holds onto the ownership of the equipment, while the lessee puts it to good use in their business. Often the lessee is given the opportunity to purchase the equipment for its market value at the end of the lease term. The main attraction of lease financing is that such borrowed items are often not included on the balance sheets of the business. Lease financing is not considered a typical debt, which means that a business in a credit crunch will have a better chance of obtaining further loans in the future if they have used lease financing than if they had borrowed it as 100 percent cash. Small businesses take advantage of lease financing often, as they do not want to hurt their relationship with their bank by using another source for cash; the bank looks upon lease financing as an acceptable alternative. Regardless, it will be a good idea to check with your bank before signing any agreements to make sure that you will not be hindering the good relationship you have worked to have with your bank.

Advantages
Allows a company to use expensive equipment without a large out-of-pocket expense.
The business holds onto a greater cash reserve.
Occasionally, the business can gain tax benefits through leasing.
It can be a constant source of cash if, after equipment is paid off, it is sold to the leaser for cash and then re-leased.
Leasing will not be a focal point on the business's financial sheets.
Generally, leasing arrangements will not harm the "one-on-one" relationship with your bank.

Disadvantages
Some loans will involve money down on the equipment for up to 20 percent of the total cost.

Sometimes a deal can be struck where the original owner retains much of the control, while the second party is involved mostly in consulting. But in general, the partner usually wants their fair share in the decisions and actions of the business. This is the reason why it becomes particularly important to know who your investors are and make sure that they are a good fit for your vision of the business. It is possible that an unfit investor could lead to the entire downfall of a company if they cause financial problems through poor communication, mismanagement, and weak customer relations.

One of the most important aspects of deciding on an equity financing transaction is deciding how much of the business you want to offer and what the exact value of that percentage should be. This is when we say to make sure that, no matter how many investors you decide to bring aboard, you retain at least 51 percent of the business. This is to ensure that you will not lose control of the business to any party or number of merging parties. The base value of each share will be determined by the current value of the business percentage, based on a thorough and unbiased valuation of accounts and projected income. This is generally accomplished by a neutral accountant who does not have a vested interest in either of the parties or general stock in the company.

Equity transactions

One way to obtain OPM is to offer equity, or stock, in your business. This is a stake in the future of your business, with investors taking a longer-range view regarding their investment until things are on the upswing. In return for their long-range view, they are hoping for a healthy return on their investment. For the business owner, it is a way to quickly raise money needed to move the business forward. It differs from a loan in that the business owner will not have an immediate cost for the money, whereas with a loan, the payments would begin almost immediately. When you offer equity in your business, you are allowing your investors to become part-owner in your enterprise. It also differs from a loan in that you are giving up a portion of your autonomy by taking on an equity investor. Now, your decisions are not your own — you have to take into account your investor's interests in any transaction you want to enter because business decisions affect their fortunes in the long run.

Equity transactions should be governed by an agreement that clearly spells out the expectations of the arrangement. Whatever arrangement you arrive at, be sure to retain majority ownership in your own business, or you could find yourself outside its doors. *Refer to Chapter 4 for a discussion of the securities laws that govern equity transactions.*

Friends, family, and employees

It is likely that you have heard the phrase "the good, the bad, and the ugly" tossed around. This phrase could be said to describe the situation of going into business with any family member. While this may seem to be one of the easiest methods to obtain OPM, especially if you have a family member who has cash stashed away, this type of loan comes with its own costs and benefits that need to be considered.

On the positive side, most family members — assuming you have a good relationship — know they can trust you and are open to giving you the opportunity to explain your business plan. You have already developed a relationship with them and should have an idea what it will be like working together — both the good and bad aspects. Family can be forgiving when it comes to paying back the amount you borrowed. Also, they will not be a threat when it comes to buying out your interest at some point in the future of your business as a venture investor might be apt to do.

With that said, let us dive into some of the bad that comes with mixing family and finances. There is a reason why most of us do not live with our extended family, and that has to do with our desire to be our own masters and make our own decisions. Adults who have had the opportunity to live with their parents can vouch for how hard it can be to be thrown into a situation of house rules once again. Even though they are adults, they are expected to live by the rules of their parents because they live under their roof. This is the same scenario that can happen when you access OPM via your family members.

When an entrepreneur uses family for investment dollars, their personal finances and purchases are no longer just their business because they have now tied themselves to that family member and they will — for lack of a better way of phrasing it — be living under someone else's roof. For example, if you owe a family member $100,000, and you decide to take your family on a Walt Disney World vacation, you can imagine what may happen. That vacation is no longer your own business because that family member will see the trip as being part of the money you owe them. They will feel it is their right to tell you whether you should be able to take that vacation and how much you should spend on other aspects of your life. Going into business with a family member is not good or bad, but it can lead to a lot of pressure and ill-feeling in a family. There is an old saying that claims you should never mix business with pleasure — or even family.

> **$ Investors' Insight:**
> There is no such thing as paying something back "when you can," even when family is involved. If it is purely a business deal, then it is a good decision to use it as a source of OPM, but you should look at this as a business deal while keeping in mind the other aspects that can crop up due to their close familial ties with you.

Combining money with family is one of the most common reasons why some mothers and sons do not speak to each other, why brothers and sisters might no longer send Christmas cards, and why holiday dinners are spent less with an extended family and more with your own family and close friends. Countless stories have been told of family who have broken ties over money. Inheritances are especially a big source of the ugliness. Many families have been divided over the unfortunate death of a loved one. If there is a large inheritance, then in some families the event is no longer about grieving but rather about who gets how much money and what items they deserve. It is something to keep in mind: When mixing money and family, it may not turn out as well as you had hoped. You will want to consider whether you want to put your familial relationships to that kind of a test.

Let us move on to another realm of borrowing: the borrowing of resources, rather than cash — otherwise known as OPR (other people's resources), as it provides uncountable benefits.

OPR: Your Other Choice

By now, you should be able to see that OPM is a great strategic choice when attempting to launch an idea that is beyond your financial means. Today, there are not very many big ideas you can bring to life with only $200,000 of your own equity to spend. The problem is there will not always be opportunities to receive $1 million in cash in order for you to push your dreams into reality. Cash is a big deal, and unless you can show a track record of profits, which is hard to do with a start-up business, most investors will not part with it easily. In these situations, there is another option for you to consider: asking for the use of investors' available resources to help build up your business. This is taking advantage of other people's resources, or OPR.

OPR can make a lot of sense for a business. Basically, you are doing away with the middleman, which in this case happens to be cash, and you get right to the object of desire, which are the resources to make your business venture a viable reality. And if you think that what you really need for a successful start-up are things beyond what most people have as available resources, think again. Whatever you can find in this world that someone else uses — whether it is distribution, sales personnel, laborers, reputation, software, a database, office/production space, equipment, or advertising — you can gain access to borrow it as a resource in exchange for another resource, cash, or an equity stake. A perfect example of such an exchange is in the bartering of toy manufacturing rights for each of George Lucas's films that are produced today.

Before the release of each of Lucas's films, he is traditionally bombarded with offers from Hasbro Inc. and Mattel Inc. to use their toy manufacturing facilities and resources to create his line of toys. These companies battle for exclusive rights to the product line by giving him offers for royalties of more than 15 percent and often a percentage of equity in the company. The nice part about such an exchange is no one really loses any out-of-pocket cash, and everyone collects a rather sizable profit. This is just one of many examples of the creative use of OPR.

$ Investors' Insight:
OPR gives you the opportunity to be creative. A deal of any kind is simply what people agree to do, so do not dismiss an "outside the box" idea if you think it is the solution you need to move your business forward.

Perhaps one of the ultimate examples of using OPR was when Peter Pocklington acquired 50 percent of the Edmonton Oilers hockey team from Nelson Skalbania in 1976. He purchased his share with no out-of-pocket expense, but rather a diamond ring from his wife's hand, a Rolls-Royce Phaeton, and a Maurice Utrillo painting — all worth about $700,000. (Pocklington later purchased the remaining shares in 1977.) In business, there are all kinds of deals that can be made, and examples of these trades in exchange for resources have been shown through history. This form of bartering can be used for the smallest goods and services, and as this Pocklington example shows, luxury goods as well.

Another reason that OPR is so effective is its handy possibility of zeroing out the transaction so that nobody involved owes anyone else any money, because the entire transfer of funds is being done through trade. If you are lucky enough to find somebody who has a resource you desperately need, and your service happens to be something that they desperately want in return, then you have found a gold mine for your business enterprise. This is the next best thing to free money. However, you have to make sure that the service you are providing is just as valuable as the resources you are receiving; otherwise, the partnership will break down, leaving you back at the starting line looking for another source to help fund your operation and move it forward.

One reason why OPR is a good choice if you are having trouble obtaining OPM is that OPR tends to be more readily available for relatively unknown people who happen to have big ideas. In the eyes of most investors, cash is a much bigger risk when compared to them giving you some of their resources. Investors like to keep a cash cushion to give them security, and if somebody is asking them for a handful of that plush filling, they want to make sure that there will be enough left to still be seated comfortably when the year is through. This is why the criteria for building an attractive business plan are very detailed. The investor is laying out a very large sum of money and will get very little immediate return for the first few months, or even up to a year. If you can break up that investment money and disguise it within a coveted product or service of equal value, suddenly the risk becomes much less for the investor while your ability to find and have access to financing seems to double. This is exactly what OPR can do for the entrepreneur: offer a much-needed product or service without a huge out-of-pocket expense for any of the players involved in the transaction. It more closely resembles a bartering arrangement, or swap, in place of a cash outlay. Each party to the agreement is getting something they want.

You will find that there are less stringent criteria imposed for OPR than for a cash transaction. Besides the reduced risk it provides the investor, it will also cost the entrepreneur themselves less, due to the gradual investment of the money source rather than one large lump sum with interest attached. This also offers a convenient way for the co-venturer to be flexibly paid back through a percentage of the profits. They will feel like a part of the project from the beginning as it is their resources (product) going directly toward the overall plan. The OPR investor can become a sister company on some level. Equity financing goes hand-in-hand when using OPR as a source for your business. If equity in the company is not something that you as the business owner are willing to part with, then fee payments can also be arranged with a more flexible schedule than OPM. Since the draw is once again more gradual, the payback can generally be a little more gradual as well.

Finally, the legal worries that come with OPM are somewhat eased when you are dealing with OPR instead. There is much less restriction and law when it comes to borrowing a resource as opposed to offering stock shares or asking for cash.

OPC (Other People's Credit)

In some cases, you may not know of anyone with a large enough savings willing to lend cash or resources, but you most likely know someone who has good credit, such as a friend, family member, or business acquaintance. So, you can leverage their credit for your use. They take on the debt on your behalf, whether it is to sign for a loan for you or place equipment on their credit card. This is exactly the same idea as OPM, as you will have to offer an incentive for someone to take a chance with their credit on behalf of your business opportunity. You will be selling yourself to this person just as you would have if you were asking them for cash.

Something to consider: As with other people's money and resources, there is only so much credit that we can ask for. Obviously, the more overextended you become using your own credit, the less likely you are going to be able to get more credit. Using OPC gives you the opportunity to keep your portfolio clean. In this respect, OPC is kind of the ultimate source of money because not only does it give you the freedom to work with money that you would not otherwise have had, but it also will not appear on your records, giving you greater opportunity to obtain OPM elsewhere. Gaining your financing through as many sources of OPM as you can provides you with the most opportunity. You do not have to stick with just one source, and the more you spread it out, the better your chances are of having access to it in the first place.

But there is a great responsibility that goes along with using OPC. If the business does not work out, you could be putting that person's financial future in jeopardy. Do not let the prospect of using someone else's credit to finance your business allow you to feel comfortable about taking greater risks. If you play fast and loose with either someone else's money or credit, you can rest assured that the news will travel. And though every success you have may open another ten doors, keep in mind that every failure can close 100.

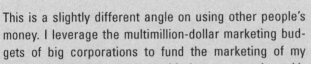

FlipScript
www.flipscript.com
Mark@FlipScript.com
Mark Hunter — President

This is a slightly different angle on using other people's money. I leverage the multimillion-dollar marketing budgets of big corporations to fund the marketing of my small technology start-ups, and it does not require asking for the money or to even have it in-hand to benefit from it. I have done this with my last two technology start-ups, and it has consistently worked out extremely well.

Of course, I use the marketing dollars of these big corporations in such a way as to not take anything away from them and, in fact, they appreciate it. I think of it as "value-added piggybacking," because once my small company has started to grow, I often help them reach their goals as well. It is an unofficial partnership of sorts, but one between a massive corporation and a tiny start-up company.

For example, in the late 1990s, when Samsung and Pioneer started to promote the idea of the flat-screen television revolution for the home, I recognized an opportunity to fill a niche for flat-screen television calibration. Calibration helps make the image more realistic than when you first purchase it "out of the box," and we created a product to make this possible.

With Samsung and Pioneer both spending millions of dollars marketing the flat-screen television revolution, I did not need to spend much at all to promote Milori Video Products. This new calibration system quickly brought the company to more than $1 million in annual sales (with high profitability) before the company was acquired in late 2004. Interestingly, both Samsung and Pioneer became big customers of the product themselves.

After selling that company, I began researching my next opportunity. When I heard that Sony Pictures would be producing the movie *Angels and Demons* for release in May 2009, I knew that their marketing would increase awareness of the ambigrams found throughout the story. Ambigrams are word designs that can be read right side-up and upside-down, and are a fascinating blend of optical illusion, typography, and psychology.

I realized that ambigrams would be the perfect way to personalize gifts for couples, since their names could be combined together into one design, and immediately began the development of a technology that could automatically create high-quality ambigrams just by typing in the two words to use in the design — the world's first ambigram generator.

CASE STUDY: FLIPSCRIPT

In late 2008, I went live with an e-commerce store at **www. FlipScript.com** to create personalized ambigram products, but spent no money on marketing or promotion. I knew that expenses would be handled for me in just a short time.

Sure enough, when Sony Pictures began to heavily market *Angels and Demons* in spring 2009, my sales shot through the roof, and again, I did not need to spend any money in promoting this unique product idea. As an added bonus, the resulting incoming hyperlinks shot **www.FlipScript.com** to the No. 1 spot in Google's search results, which increased traffic and sales still further.

Similar to the last venture, the corporation that I was "piggybacking" with became a great customer themselves when Sony Pictures came knocking just before the movie release. They signed a contract and built a new web site called AmbigramQuest to showcase our designs in order to further promote their movie (a form of reverse piggybacking). Landing the marketing host company as a customer is not the main goal, but it does seem to be a consistent side-benefit.

This unique way of using other people's marketing money has been a great way to accelerate the growth of a small company with a niche product very quickly. Best of all, you do not need to beg, plead, or even borrow to get the benefit of the money. Just look for an opportunity where there will be millions of dollars in marketing money spent in a specific area, and create something that will automatically benefit when a corporation (or corporations) increases your company's awareness for you.

Chapter 9:

Securing OPM

The Interview Process

A lot of preparation goes into starting a business, especially if you want to increase your chances of having investors want to put their money and trust in your venture. When it comes time to seek that investment money, you have all of the research you have done into the specifics of your idea and how to make it launch successfully. The research you have done will boost your confidence when you are ready to sit down and present your case. And your confidence will help a would-be investor feel more confident in giving you the money to move your idea forward. In particular, your business plan will give you an excellent foundation and garner respect for the amount of knowledgeable detail you put into it. Investors will feel more comfortable going into business with someone who has taken the pains to create a sound plan that is based on a range of research and supporting facts. It is one tool in your arsenal of tactics to obtain OPM. Another important tool is your ability to negotiate to make the deal happen.

Negotiate the Deal

Ideally, when you go to an investor to negotiate getting the funds you need for your business, you will want a one-time conversation, not a series of meetings. Timing is usually critical for a new business venture, and dealing with issues that drag out the process can sometimes close the window of opportunity before you have a chance to access it.

This is why you should spend a lot of time on the front end of building your business plan — devoting the time necessary to account for any questions from any angle that could possibly come up in an investor's mind. While you cannot account for every question that comes up, the last thing you want is to leave a negotiating table with a list of "I will check into that..." items that could delay the deal and impact your overall timeline.

When you are ready to find money to finance your business, you will want to have a clear plan as to exactly what you are going in for, as well as your negotiating plan to achieve that goal. Your negotiating tactics depend on several factors:

1. Whom you are negotiating with
2. The amount of money you need
3. Your experience level as an entrepreneur
4. The prevailing economic market

While some experts recommend grilling the bank about their competency, sometimes it is a good idea to let the lender know that you realize they are doing you a favor and that you appreciate their time and advice. Many business leaders will take you

under their wing, so to speak, because they remember being in your shoes at one point in their own careers.

In this scenario, if a lender finds that you have a questionable business plan or are on the fence for qualification, empathy can definitely play a role in receiving a loan where others may not. Commercial bankers do not have to offer a loan to everyone who qualifies. Loan approvers have the capacity to go with their gut when it comes to a potential borrower, where some who qualify are rejected because something about the deal seems off, and someone who is unqualified gets approved because they trust their instinct about the potential of the deal. There is a saying in business that people do business with those they like and trust. This means that there is much more at stake here than just your credit numbers and bottom line. However, once you have negotiated a deal and it is time to go in for a second loan, things can change by moving to the next level.

Once you can show success and a solid payment history with the first loan, you will walk into the bank with a lot more clout the next time you need a loan and, accordingly, your negotiating abilities will take on a different approach. It is all part of the growth process for a new entrepreneur, and every entrepreneur had to start out as a rookie, just like you.

Now that you have some leverage with your first successful loan, you can work the second loan for a better deal. Every bank manager is always looking to see what his or her competition is doing. If you walk in to the bank to get your second loan and you are honest with them in telling them you have found a better deal elsewhere, that is perfectly acceptable. Make sure they know you would be willing to consider any offers they would have, as you would like to stay with them. Commercial bank lending is very competitive, and sometimes you can get two banks competing to serve you. There are such times, however, when you will want to choose your battles, such as when you are negotiating fees.

Fee negotiations

Fees are an expense for your business, and they are one area in which every bank has some wiggle room. But you will need to consider the type of loan you are after before deciding if that is what you want to concentrate your negotiation tactics on. For instance, sometimes it is better to get your fees knocked down and pay a higher rate if you know that you are only going to be carrying the loan for a short-term period. On the other hand, if you are going to be in for a long-term deal, it may be all right to pay the higher fees in exchange for a substantially lower rate. The main thing to remember is to do your math when calculating out how much you will pay over the course of the loan.

Do your homework before going into any bank, as many banks will know what the competition is doing; if they do not know already, they will certainly be interested in the information. If you walk into a bank and are able to discuss the deals that you know are available with other banks, then you can tell them exactly what you are looking for. This will put you in the position of having the bank work for you, instead of your working for them, as you might have done for your first loan. This is one way to get a better deal in the end. However, this will only work for the well-prepared entrepreneur who has taken the time to do their homework and knows what they are talking about. If you walk in without any formal plan or proposal, and with no clear goal of what you want to achieve in your meeting, you are most likely going to have problems getting the loan in the first place.

Mutual Confidentiality Agreement and Letter of Intent (LOI)

If you have done your job and made the case for your business idea with your source, then at some point during the negotiations you are going to want to secure a letter of intent (LOI) from them. The LOI is not binding for the OPM source, and so as long as they are interested in your proposal and feel that it has growth and profit potential, this should not prove to be too difficult to get them to sign one. The LOI is basically saying that the company has expressed interest in being a potential partner to the entrepreneur, and they are interested in pursuing the idea further with the intent of potentially signing a deal if everything looks good.

About 50 percent of the time, you will run into a situation where the OPM source will ask for more proof to support your assessment that your planned business venture will be successful. This means that they would like you to create a detailed business plan *Refer to Chapter 7 on the elements of the successful business plan for guidance.*

Before you go through all of this work, it will be in your best interest to get some type of an agreement hammered out between the two of you. You will want an LOI describing exactly what it is that the company is looking to see from you, and you will also want a mutual confidentiality agreement (MCA). The MCA is used in conjunction with the LOI to help establish trust and the beginnings of the partnership. You would not want to bring an

idea to a company, only to find that weeks later they have part-
nered with somebody else and decided to implement your idea
with them instead. This is something of a safeguard that you are
setting up that creates a written understanding that the prospec-
tive partner will not take your information and ideas elsewhere.
If they will not sign one of these with you, you should be wary of
their intentions with your business ideas because these letters are
not binding for them. They either have little interest on their part
to begin with in your plan, or they see its potential and want to
run with it for themselves.

Most companies will honor both the LOI and MCA without question. News of any poor business practices travels fast, and companies like to pride themselves on having reputations built on
honor and integrity. The only way the typical company would
break a confidentiality agreement is if during the time of your negotiations, somebody else came up with the exact same concept
and brought the same idea to their attention. At this point, it is no
longer considered confidential, and your idea might be released
through various sources.

This is the reason why you should never sit on an idea for any
given amount of time. There is no guarantee that somebody else
would not think of the same thing and act faster than you. If you
have a hot idea, you would want to jump on it while it is still
fresh and unclaimed.

Many times a company may tell you that the MCA will be sufficient for you to continue into the research phase of the negotiations, but it will be in your best interests to press for an LOI.
If need be, you can tell them that in order for you to proceed to

your research phase — which will take both time and money — you need a commitment from them. Without a commitment of some sort, it is far easier for somebody to turn you down. An LOI can also help to basically weed out the companies who are truly interested from the ones who may be only curious. The LOI essentially says that if you are able to come up with the agreed-upon information that the company has deemed necessary to continue negotiations, then a contract may be signed between the two parties.

Without insisting on this type of protection for yourself, you run the risk of wasting time researching specific questions for one company, and if they turn you down, you would have to research the next group's list of questions. Again, a solid business plan from the outset can alleviate a lot of those questions that could potentially come up, so thoroughness early on pays dividends in time saved when you are ready to move.

With this being said, in all fairness we should look at the reasons why some venture capitalists would not want to sign any preliminary agreements. Venture capitalists often receive many proposals a day for new ideas that run the gamut, ranging from Internet music distribution to cell phone services. With all of these ideas, it is difficult for the venture capitalist to keep up on all the agreements. If they were to read through and sign every agreement of interest that came across their desk, it would take precious hours. In addition to this, they are under the gun to some degree.

If they were to sign an LOI with one entrepreneur who was unable to submit substantial proof of their idea, and somebody else comes along with a similar idea and was able to give sufficient evidence, then they are in essence backed into a business corner. They now face the possibility of a lawsuit from the other individual claiming that they stole their idea. This lets you see what the investor's perspective is; it is a good reason why each case should be decided on an individual basis.

One such scenario is that, when dealing with the possibility of investments from several companies, you can use the MCA and LOI to bait each of the companies to commit further in order to gain more information on the other partners. They will naturally want to know who the other partnering companies are so they can research their capabilities. But as with all good business practice, you cannot give out such information until the confidentiality and commitment agreement has been signed. Once signed, you can arrange a meeting between all partners where further negotiations may commence.

The initial draft of your MCA and LOI should not be too lengthy or complicated. It should not be binding in any way, but rather express a commitment of trust and understanding between all parties. There are resources on the Web, but you may want to check with your attorney about drafting one that is specific to your business interests.

Contract Considerations

If you went into your negotiation with a plan for the desired outcome, then you know whether or not the contract you are about to sign meets those goals. There are several areas you will want to decide on before you ever get to the negotiating table.

Questions for which you will want to know the answer ahead of time include:

1. What is my limit for how much I want to spend as part of the cost of doing business?

2. What fees do I feel are negotiable?

3. When looking at terms and conditions, where am I willing to negotiate, and what do I consider to be non-negotiable?

4. How much of a stake in my business am I willing to give up to an investor?

5. What would make me walk away from the negotiating table?

And then there are the unknowable questions, the most important one being, "What does the other side want out of this deal?" Obviously, when you are at the negotiation table, there are two sides to it: the entrepreneur with his or her wants and needs, and the investor who has his or her own wants and needs. Here are some questions to consider the range of possible scenarios for when it comes to potential investors:

1. What type of return on investment might they be looking for?

2. What would sway this investor to want to provide money for my deal?

3. Would this investor be interested in a stake in the company?

4. Is there some special knowledge or experience the investor could gain from investing in my venture?

5. Whom has this investor worked with before?

6. What is this investor's background?

7. What strengths and weaknesses does this investor have?

A lot of these questions will not be answerable until you are actually sitting with the investor. Although you have come prepared with your ideas and supporting research, also remember to make a conscious effort to *listen* to the investor. This will provide you with a lot of clues as to how to negotiate more than focusing a torrent of words at the investor in hopes of selling them on your idea.

CASE STUDY: PRUDENTIAL GEORGIA REALTY

Prudential Georgia Realty
www.cmsells.com
cmsellsga@gmail.com
Phone: (770) 598-7771
Christa Michael — Associate Broker

I first heard about using OPM for promotion of my business in July 2000. I had attended a real estate convention and saw that some other realtors were doing it and thought: *Why not me?*

Even though I heard about it in 2000, it took me a while to get the nerve to do it myself. I had been in real estate since 1997 and really had not learned how to market myself without spending my own money. As a new realtor, I did not have the money to get my name out there, either. In February 2001, I finally took the plunge. I bought a 17-foot moving truck that my clients could use — for free. I financed it and had it paid off in six months using OPM.

My greatest fear was asking for the money. I really felt I had nothing to offer people in exchange for their money. Boy, was I wrong. Today, I have zero fears about asking to use OPM. When I show my sources what the benefit is and what they will get in return, they are all for it. The best advice I can give someone wanting to use OPM to market or get their business going is to just do it. The worst that can happen is they will say no. If they do, go on to the next person.

When I first started scouting for OPM sources, I looked for companies to participate with me that were in my industry or related to it. Then I found that a lot of smaller companies do not have the money to do big advertising, so with their money, they get more exposure than they could normally afford on their own. It is a win-win for all. Now I am open to approaching everyone and anyone.

You really have to view using OPM that everyone will get something out of the deal. You have to make it work for all parties, and you want everyone to be happy. To make sure that your investors are happy, keep in contact with them. Track what kind of business they are getting and modify what you need to make sure they are getting a good return on their investment. Communication is the key. This is your reputation as well that you are putting on the line. If you cannot deliver, then you need to find other benefits for OPM that you are using. For me and my investors, having this partnership meant more exposure, more business, more affiliations, and more contacts.

If you have never used OPM before, or you are just starting out in your industry, you may receive a little bit of resistance. But, if you are an open-minded thinker and can think outside the box, you will succeed. You have to do something and

CASE STUDY: PRUDENTIAL GEORGIA REALTY

provide something that no one else in your industry or your area is offering to make it work.

Every time that I have had to go to an OPM source, I have had my ducks in a row. You have to put yourself in their situation, and you should be able to answer their questions, like: How much money do you want from me a month? What am I getting in return? What kind of exposure are you go ing to give my business? What if I am not happy? What if I find that I am spending more with you than I am earning?

Using OPM can be a great thing, but it really must be a win-win for all. You can definitely expect flack from your competitors when they see you doing some different things, but do not let that deter you. You decided how successful you want to be, and you control your own destiny. If you really want something, you need to make it happen. Using OPM is a great way to get to the top fast.

Chapter 10:

Managing OPM

You Have the Money — Now What?

You have done your research on your business idea, located and negotiated with investors, and secured them as sources of OPM to get your business launched. Now what?

This is where some businesses can go astray: by relaxing now that the money is in their hands. However, even a slight pause can slow down the momentum in getting your business up and into a successful position for profitability. The owner may wake up one day and find that his or her company has derailed somewhere along the way with no idea how it could have happened. There are some common snags that new companies can get caught up in.

One of the biggest issues that can lead to failure of the business venture is if the company does not actually make use of the business plan they worked so diligently to create. It has been slipped into a leather binder and placed on a shelf. Your business plan is not meant to be enshrined in a museum. It should be treated as a living document and used as a navigational tool to guide your business operations. Use it as a weekly, or even daily, reminder of what the company's goals are. Remember that the business plan can be tweaked and revised as your venture progresses and matures. Your projections will change as you are doing business, learning firsthand how your market works, seeing how your distribution channels function, and reviewing any other factors that can affect your operation.

You sold your investors on your vision, and now it is time to deliver on what you said you could do. You have the money and are responsible for giving your absolute best effort in bringing the return on investment that you projected in your business plan. Your dreams are just as important as your investors' expectations: Never lose sight of where you started. You had a dream to create wealth and breathe your ideas into a living reality. Now that you have your opportunity, the last thing you want to do is squander it.

> **$ Investors' Insight:**
> A best practice you can incorporate into your business is putting a business meeting regularly on the calendar — even if it is only you in attendance. Take the time to evaluate the business often. By setting aside the time away from the daily operation, your mind may relax enough to come up with creative solutions or to gain insight into specific issues that the business is facing.

We will go over some key questions you will want to know the answers to so that at any given time, you know the state of your business. These questions are based on what you developed in your business plan and will serve to guide you in staying on point or making the necessary course corrections.

Marketing analysis

1. What different avenues are you using for your marketing and advertising?

2. Which advertising methods are bringing you the best return on your investment — which, in this case, would be your clients?

3. What are you learning about your target market that you have to allow for in your marketing plan?

4. Have any competitors moved into your market?

Financial analysis

1. Are you meeting your financial projections?

2. Where do you need to spend more time and resources?

3. Have costs changed, and how are you budgeting for them?

4. Where are the peaks and dips occurring in your business?

5. Do you have enough working capital to carry you through the month, the quarter, and the year?

These are the types of questions you will constantly want to ask as you analyze your business operations. You will find that markets change constantly, and you will want to ensure that your business is nimble enough to maneuver through those changes.

How To Structure Your "Debt" to Get the Most out of a Deal

The best way to structure your debt is to hold on to as much of your own money as possible, allowing that money to work for you. By using OPM, either borrowing through a line of credit or assets, you will be able to retain your own funds and leverage them as needed.

A bank is more inclined to loan money to people who already have some money than to someone who does not have any. This is one of the biggest reasons why it is never a good idea to tap your own resources and spend that money until it dwindles down to almost nothing before seeking additional funding. You never want to use your own money when other sources of funds are available to you.

For example, if you go into your bank where you currently have a balance of $200,000 and ask to borrow $100,000, the bank manager is more likely to do business with you; but if you started with a balance of $200,000 and spent all but $20,000 of it, your chances of getting more money have probably evaporated. Even if you have excellent credit, it may not be enough to compensate for the fact that you have no existing capital. This is why it is so important to hold on to as much of your personal capital as possible, because it is a means of leveraging. Just because you have the money does not mean you have to spend it before seeking more, and you will be much better off in the long run for seeking other sources with which to spend.

Debt is an interesting phenomenon, wherein sometimes it is actually better to go into debt to borrow money while you still have a large chunk of money in the bank. Overall, this can be a much better business decision than using all of your own money and never having any debt. The difference is that while the one entrepreneur will be debt-free, he or she will also be limited in the amount of extra funds at their disposal, because they do not have the security they could have had if they had spent someone else's money instead. When you are dealing with OPM, you might want to re-think how you view debt. It is not always a bad situation to be in, and it may actually be your strength in the end. You will always have your own assets as a last resort, which will make you evaluate how much you are willing to put on the line for your business.

Marketing

Above, there were listed some questions to ask as you move through your business cycle. The one aspect of OPM that can be extremely effective to boost almost any idea and business is marketing. Marketing can be an expensive project for a new business to use to its fullest capacity if you lack an open source of cash from which to spend. Intense marketing can make the difference between being a business that is booming in two years or a business that is forced into bankruptcy. It is not uncommon for a new business to have to spend an enormous portion of their budget to successfully market itself for a year — especially the first year. Add on the available cash needed to keep the business afloat while it is gaining clients, and it is easy to see how a large amount of funds from which to draw could make a big difference. It is not only the money that brings you the clients, but also the strategy used along with the money that will be your most effective tool.

In your business plan, you will make projections on how you plan to market your service, product, or idea. Once you are in business, you have the hard evidence of your sales numbers to analyze how those original projections are working for you, as was touched on in the marketing questions listed earlier. Analysis should be ongoing, as effective marketing and advertising is the life of your company's profitability. No matter what your business venture is, profits do not happen in a vacuum. The ideas behind your company need to be constantly put out front before your target market because they have a short attention span and are bombarded constantly with offers of all kinds. You can guarantee that if you are not aggressive in your advertising efforts, your competitors will be.

Boosting Sales

Most successful business people would say that what is essential for gaining sales is creativity, strategy, and the ability to think outside the box. Such ideas usually fall under these six simple theories:

- Understand the customer/client and their needs

- Use strategic marketing campaigns and track their success

- Make profit awareness should be part of every marketing strategy

- Use viral marketing and branding to boost sales

- Keep your message and service simple for the customer

- Build your service and product with quality

The real key here is not only what lies outside the box, but being mindful of what is happening on the inside, which is the reality

of what a business is capable of and can actually be expected to accomplish using these guidelines.

Understand the clients and their needs

Building a strong relationship with the client is the cornerstone to boosting sales, and you do this by getting to know your customers on a level that moves beyond just the buy-sell relationship. You do this by asking them about things that are not related to business. Questions you can ask include those about their background, such as where they grew up and where they went to school, what they like to do on the weekends, or questions about their kids' activities. These types of questions build that all-important rapport, where people do business with one another because they have a genuine "like" for that person. Trust and loyalty are built in this way. It will also give you a window into the lives of your customers, helping you to see the challenges they face and the types of problems they need solved.

Use and track strategic marketing campaigns

Albert Einstein defined insanity as "doing the same thing over and over again and expecting different results." If sales are suffering, it is time to step back and take a look at how you are going about your marketing.

Examine your budget and make sure you have allocated sufficient funds to marketing. This does not mean it is a wise course to spend your business into a hole in an effort to boost sales. You will want to review your strategies to see if you have set yourself sufficiently apart from your competition by claiming a niche and maximizing your exposure there.

When it comes to the advice of working outside the box, think small on your initial campaigns, then track how well they do for you. There is no point in pouring a ton of your marketing dollars into something that will bring you a minimal return on your investment. Test each strategy you use, wait for the results, analyze them, and decide if you want to move forward — then invest more in that strategy or move on. The key is to keep track of every dollar you have spent in marketing and gauge how much you have received back on that dollar.

You will also want to evaluate your advertising efforts before you sign an advertising contract so that you are not investing your OPM on advertising that you find is not right for your business, but are now bound to contractually. Study what your competition is doing and whether their strategies are effective. Also, consider if the strategies you are interested in are a good fit for your business. Not every advertising venue is appropriate for every business. A billboard or a magazine advertisement may not fit with the type of service or product you are offering, so you will save yourself time, effort, and marketing dollars by weighing in advance the different options available to your business.

Profit awareness should be part of every marketing strategy

This builds on strategizing your marketing and keeping an eye on your return on investment. You want to make sure you have set an appropriate budget but do not overextend the ability of the business to receive a return. There is a tipping point where the law of diminishing returns kicks in, so you want to be well ahead of that. Diminishing returns occur when the market becomes saturated with a product or a service, outpacing the demand; the company will then reach a peak in their ability to make a profit for the investment they have made in putting their products or services on the market. You have to know when to push forward and when to pull back, and this requires being mindful of trends, effectiveness of your marketing strategies, and economic factors. A lot of this will have been found during the discovery process as you were building your business plan, and this is why it is crucial to keep that plan handy and work to keep it updated as frequently as possible.

By asking themselves a few simple questions, a business can strategically build on a plan to boost sales without overextending themselves. These are the key questions to look at:

1. Will this endeavor bring increased revenue by highlighting your product or service in a new way?

2. Is the time it will take to land the sale worth the profit?

3. Is this endeavor measurable?

4. Is the marketing strategy just following an untested trend, or is it a trend that will bring results?

5. Does the business have the resources and capacity to handle a large influx of sales?

Track your ROI

When you put money or time into something, generally you expect to get something out of it. This is called return on investment, or ROI. The basic calculation for figuring your ROI is:

((Payback − Investment)/Investment) × 100

There is more to this formula, especially for the small business. Do not forget to put a number to how much an hour of your time is worth because it is the equivalent of sweat equity; time an owner can put into his or her business is an often unchampioned investment in the business enterprise. The idea that one's time is often every bit as valuable as money is sometimes forgotten by the small business owner. There are more time pressures on the one- or two-person operation than on a larger business, where tasks can be spread out among multiple people. If you are expending an enormous amount of time to gain a profit, you will need to calculate how much your time is worth to see if you are getting a good return on your time, as well as cash outlay.

For example, let us say you owned a pizza business and decided to place a flier about your business and the pizza deals you are offering in every residential door in the zip code where your business is. Though you may be able to run off a thousand or more fliers for a decent price, if you are the only one walking around and delivering them— and it takes the better part of two weeks — you have to weigh how good your return will be on not just the cost of the fliers, but the amount of time you invested in delivering them. In this case, doing them as mail inserts may be more cost-effective and bring you a greater return on your investment than hand-delivering them. Of course, if you are a start-up company, there may be a time period when all you have to offer your business at the moment is your sweat equity — maybe while you are waiting for investors to accept your request for funds. Instead of letting your business plans lie fallow, you will want to spend your sweat equity in the interim in order to get your business rolling on its own or when those funds do arrive, and get your business into a position where you can move to a more profitable level of marketing that increases your return without costing you time.

Using viral marketing and branding to boost sales

There are some great, time-saving ways you can take advantage of to market your business. Two of the most cost-effective and savvy marketing strategies available to today's technology-hungry consumers are viral marketing and branding. These tools will be particularly effective for local consumer products and services, as well as national e-commerce-based small businesses.

Viral marketing

Viral marketing is essentially a term that refers to common phrases such as "word-of-mouth," "creating a buzz," "leveraging the media," and "network marketing." It is best described as a voice that you can use to promote your business by allowing others to experience your product or Web site. If your product or service is good and people talk about your product, news will spread like a virus. Basically, it is free marketing. When you provide a good product or service, are reliable, and solve people's problems, those customers will want to share their good fortune and finding with others.

Three steps to viral marketing

1. **Give away a valuable product or service:** This attracts attention to your service and allows people to see the kind of product or service you provide.

2. **Use existing communication networks**: Place your marketing message within your network of businesses,

friends, and family, and ask them to pass it on. This allows it to filter down and into other networks.

3. **Offer the market the easiest method for your message to be transferred:** Can you describe what you sell in 30 seconds or fewer, or fit it onto a business card or e-mail to various clients and acquaintances?

Branding

Branding is not just about getting consumers to choose your product or service over the competition. Instead, branding is about persuading them to view your product or service as the only one that can provide a transformation toward a solution that will change their life or business for the better. The goal is to have your product or service become synonymous with the want or need that the consumer is looking for.

The American Marketing Association (AMA) defines branding as a "name, term, sign, symbol or design, or a combination of them intended to identify the goods and services of one seller or group of sellers and to differentiate them from those of other sellers." To effectively brand yourself, you must know what it is that your target consumer needs and wants, and find a way to symbolize your understanding of that.

These techniques can be used for more than just the budding business attempting to gain visibility and sales. Sometimes an established but ailing business may need to reinvigorate itself through re-branding. A perfect example of this is TYLENOL®, which was hit with a negative brand association after the infamous poison scare of 1982, when seven people died after ingesting capsules laced with cyanide.

Sometimes, it is effective to reach the audience you are marketing to by putting your business on the same level as the consumer, such as Allstate's slogan of "You're in good hands." This gives them the aura of a kindly friend looking out for you. Other times, it can be by appearing larger than life, creating a sort of celebrity status or air of exclusivity that makes people want to aspire to what you are offering. Think of luxury brand items— and even non-luxury items — that have become synonymous with what purpose they serve:

- **Rolex** — A watch
- **Chanel** — High fashion
- **Kleenex** — Tissue
- **Google** — Internet search
- **Xerox** — Photocopy

The ABC television hit *Dancing with the Stars* has created huge opportunities for dance studios around the world, in particular the Arthur Murray Franchise Dance Studios. "Anyone can dance like the stars at Arthur Murray's" is their branding slogan. Since the show began in 2005, the Murray studios have been making a great deal of money because people want to learn to dance like the stars they are seeing on the television show — and Arthur Murray is making that promise in their slogan. The lesson of these examples is that if you can find a way to connect your brand to your customers' personal lives, needs, and dreams, your sales are almost guaranteed to increase in return.

If you cannot find something in existence to connect your brand to, then create your own. Nike Inc. gained instant respect for its brand of golf balls after one infamous stroke of luck by pro golfer Tiger Woods. He dropped a ball with the Nike logo into the hole at the Masters Golf Tournament in Georgia. A new leading brand of golf ball was instantly born.

Keep your message and service simple for the customer

You should craft a simple, straightforward marketing message; you want to stick with the basics, keeping your marketing strategies concise. Some estimates show that the brain wanders every seven seconds before returning to a task, and experts say that television has conditioned people to only be able to hold their attention for about 10 to 15 minutes, almost the length of a segment before going to commercial. On the Web, you only have a few seconds to hook a reader before they grow impatient and move along. It is these types of statistics you will want to keep in mind when working on your marketing materials.

Long, complicated explanations will quickly lose the consumer, as they simply do not have the time to decipher an overload of information. Do the work for them by breaking down your offerings in as basic a format as possible. You want to give the essence of your business, distilled down to its bare bones to show how the consumer will benefit from doing business with you and how you will solve their problems. You can always offer access to additional resources for anyone who would like more in-depth information. Figure out what the "hook" is for your business, which can be described as the honey that draws the bees. For example, Nike Inc. has built their branding on just three words: "Just do it." They did not burden their market with information on the intricacies of how a running shoe is made, or how the fibers are woven to make a shoelace. Instead, Nike Inc. used a simple message that inspired people to do business with them. When you are working on your marketing message or working with a marketing firm, think in sound bites: a captured thought that encapsulates your business, quickly and easily said with minimal words.

People not only do business with people they like, but they also prefer to go with the business that makes the act of doing business *easy*. If you overcomplicate the ability to do business, customers are more inclined to walk away and find someone else whom they can easily hand their money over to. Provide quality service and products, and you will gain customer gratitude, which translates into loyalty to your company — and word-of-mouth advertising.

Above all, build your service and product with quality

Think about the companies and business people you have dealt with as a consumer and consider what impressed you most about some, as well as what turned you off in others. Obviously, you will want to mimic the qualities of those who impressed you.

Ask your friends, family, and neighbors what drives them crazy about a person or company they are trying to do business with, and the majority of the time you will hear complaints regarding the lack of customer service. This can translate into not delivering on promises, not calling back when supposed to, and even how the phone is answered. How about those companies you call where you have an automated attendant you are unable to sidestep, no matter how many numbers you press? If you want to effectively negate all of your marketing efforts and kill your business, then try out some of those tactics. It is a sure bet that you will drive away your prospects and clients in droves. Again, it is about how easy you make it for people to do business with you; no one wants to jump through hoops in order to hand over their money to your company.

If you want to get and keep clients, then put their needs and satisfaction first in everything you do. Profits tend to follow sound business practices, and one of the hallmarks of a good business is one that takes care of people. If you are unsure of how to go about it, study successful companies and see what you can learn from their best practices. To break it down to its simplest components, your business should strive to uphold the Golden Rule: Treat others as you want to be treated. People want to do business with people they feel have their best interests at heart.

Subcontract Overseas for Services

This is not a very popular stance from the perspective of people who see their jobs being outsourced to other countries, but to the business owner, outsourcing may be one of very few options they have to get their business running and profitable. This is especially true if the entrepreneur is having difficulty securing adequate funds from their sources of OPM, or if they need to keep their costs down to maximize what OPM they do have.

The Outsourcing Institute (**www.outsourcing.com**) is a professional association for those who are interested in the business of outsourcing. It is one source that an entrepreneur on a budget may want to look into in order to keep within a tight budget while managing their OPM. Membership is free, and they provide information and networking resources. But outsourcing has certainly been under scrutiny by legislature and is a fine line to ride in some instances. Security law is one such instance, and this is due to some of the sensitive information that a company may be giving the other country to process. Information concerning medical records, financial records, payroll, social security, and employees is deemed private and therefore falls under the watchful eye of the global privacy laws. Not only must the business doing the outsourcing follow these rules, but it is also their responsibility to make sure that the source to whom they are outsourcing is complying with those rules, as well.

Here in the United States, businesses are subject to the Gramm-Leach-Bliley Act (GLB). The basic GLB model states three requirements:

1. The business must ensure the security and confidentiality of all customer information.

2. The business must protect the customer from any unauthorized access to their information that may lead to potential danger or inconvenience.

3. The business must protect the information itself from the threat of being accessed and altered in any way.

In addition, the company must:

1. Designate a particular employee to assess these security laws.

2. Identify any possible risks to the customer's information and then implement safeguards for each of them.

3. Design a program to test the security of the system.

4. Select a responsible and trustworthy service provider.

5. Constantly update and reevaluate circumstances to keep everything protected.

The real threat to outsourcing today is legislation. In 2004, federal anti-offshore-outsourcing legislation was on the table threatening to ban private companies to which the government had outsourced work from, in turn outsourcing that work offshore to other countries. It was not passed, so there has not been any legislation that has been allowed to limit outsourcing to private entities, such as the individual or small business, in any way. This does not make outsourcing necessarily free and clear, as there is now a chance that state legislature may be able to slow down this process in the future, especially when economic stakes are being closely scrutinized. While they may not be able to stop it, they could certainly take some of the wind out of the sail.

The complexities of outsourcing are beyond the scope of this book, so it is simply recommended that you as the entrepreneur surround yourself with the necessary experts, such as an attorney or a consulting firm that specializes in outsourcing, to guide you through this process if you are considering it as a solution for your business needs. A knowledgeable lawyer is a must, but so is an advisor who is well-versed in the securities laws of outsourcing. Again, the Outsourcing Institute mentioned earlier provides a storehouse of information. Outsourcing can be a great way to spend your OPM frugally, but make sure that you have covered all your bases before you step into this territory.

You Are Your Own Best Investment Manager

Because OPM allows the entrepreneur to keep a cash cushion in their bank, many may be tempted to invest a portion for further gain. If you are considering dabbling in the markets, remember that there are a lot of investment strategies today that claim they can turn just about anyone into a multi-millionaire. The sad truth regarding many investment theories is that the teachers of these programs are merely failed investors themselves who have only become millionaires by the millions of folks who have purchased their plan explaining the "secrets" on how to get rich. Although some of the investment strategies are at least partially truth-based, many amount to little more than scams. The only one who seems to get rich is the one who came up with the scheme in the first place. The most glaring recent example is the Ponzi scheme masterminded by Bernie Madoff, who brought investors in with the promise of large returns. He had to keep bringing investors in to pay off the earlier investors, and so on, until it eventually came tumbling down like a house of cards. In the Madoff scandal, the estimated total loss for thousands of clients was around $65 billion.

Michael Edesess, author of *The Big Investment Lie,* tells us where most investments create their greatest fortunes: through their investor, meaning, it may not be worth it to you financially to use an investment manager to help you invest your money. One of the best overall investment strategies out there is for someone to become an investment manager. "The best way to make money is to let people think that you are doing something really smart for them," Edesess said. *Learn more about Edesess, who is covered more fully in the case study at the end of Chapter 12.*

So, what can you do if you do not want to rely on professional help with your investing? Because investing is essentially luck-based, Edesess recommends investing in small amounts using index funds. These will not give you the substantial gains that some of the riskier investments can, but they are safe, profitable, and something that anyone can take advantage of with their own money.

Another opportunity for smart, self-guided investments is with technology companies, such as Intuitive Surgical, Inc. (ISRG) ISRG makes the robotic surgery device known as the da Vinci® Surgical System, which performs precision surgeries (open-heart surgery), without the need of traditional invasive measures.

There are trend companies, such as the Trends Research Institute (**www.trendsresearch.com**), PSFK (**www.psfk.com**), and WGSN (**www.wgsn.com**), that research the latest ideas that are going on in business, technology, and culture, and make forecasts as to what the next trends may be. Trend companies are where the best opportunities can be found because they make it their business, and the more obvious the trend, such as those found in technology, the less chance you have of being wrong. The trick is to recognize when to get in on and when to get out of a trend on the upswing.

If you work with a mentor, they can save you years of learning the hard way by sharing the tricks they have learned on their investment path. Read widely and stay current on what is going on in the news and what industries are being favored by the government or what companies are giving consumers what they want and need and earning handsome dividends in the process.

Managing the Cost of Credit

Although most of the experts will tell you that it is almost always better to use other people's money instead of your own, there are times when the cost of credit is just not worth it over the long term. Consider the ramifications of paying 16 percent interest on a loan compared with the option of paying off the loan using your own money that is sitting in the bank accruing a mere 4 to 5 percent interest. In this case, it would be to your financial advantage to use your own money to pay off the OPM loan. You must always be conscious of managing your debt. This refers to keeping a close eye on your percentage of interest paid out versus your percentage of the profits using the OPM. If a source begins to cost you more than you are receiving a profit on, then you will need to pay off that debt with either your own money or an alternative source of OPM. Debt is a revolving cost and therefore must be managed and evaluated on a continual basis to make sure that you are getting the best interest rates possible at all times.

Something else to consider is that the more an entrepreneur borrows, the more overextended they may become, and therefore, they may have a more difficult time finding loans from sources, especially traditional ones, such as a bank. Your credit score, as we have looked at already, is of the utmost importance, so you should strive to maintain as high a score as possible. There will be times when credit is your best avenue in securing a loan, and other times when it is to your best advantage to pay off a project using your own money.

Credit is a balancing act of interest rates and cash flow. If the OPM that you need to borrow is going to create a significant cash flow, and the only loan you can attain has a rather high interest rate, it may still be worth it. If you are working on a deal that will create a smaller cash flow, you will have to decide if the interest rate and costs associated with the loan will be less than the money made. It is a common mistake among new business owners to borrow without first thinking through the entire process to make sure that the end result is worth it. If not, then you may need to investigate other areas of OPM or an entirely different venture altogether. Always ask yourself this question: How much money is it going to cost me to make money?

Raise the Bar

The importance of regularly reviewing your business plan cannot be stressed enough. It is your guide to success. And as such, it will require updating as you move through the year. Getting ready to go into business is a lot different than actually being in business, where dreams meet reality. There will be factors that you did not foresee that will affect your business, whether it is a change in the economy, fuel prices, consumer tastes, or some combination of all of these. Whether you are building your wealth with real estate or through a product you are offering, you can guarantee that the business landscape will change from where it was when you initiated your business plan.

If while reviewing your plan you find that everything is on track according to your projections, then it may be time to consider raising the bar on your expectations for the business earlier than you had planned. Evaluate the numbers and see if you can set higher goals to strive for. This can bring you greater profits with which to pay down debt, expand your existing enterprise, turn it into a franchise, or launch an entirely new business. Also, it is beneficial for you to be able to show future investors and sources of OPM that your business was able to exceed its projections by a positive percentage. The very act of doing well in business can be used as further leverage in attaining your goals.

CASE STUDY: THE CASH FLOW MERCENARY

The Cash Flow Mercenary
P.O. Box 250203
Franklin, MI 48025
Phone: (248) 470-8170
http://CashFlowMercenary.com
dennis.fassett@gmail.com
Follow Dennis on Twitter: @dennisfassett
Dennis Fassett — Michigan Real Estate Investor & Landlord

I started using OPM when the bottom started to drop in the automotive industry. Where I originally had been on the high-rolling track to becoming vice president of a major automotive supplier, my company was soon heaving in the financial throes caused by the plummeting industry. My department was eliminated, and instead of the title of vice president, I found myself reassigned to a different department entirely. To add to my financial burden, company stock was sinking. In short, I lost my shirt.

With a family and a big mortgage to support, I needed to do something fast. I began doing research, starting with a home equity loan, then moved on to develop a large amount of unsecured business credit, then seller financing, and finally using private investor's money to fund my deals.

To locate private investors, I started out using direct mail and other types of broadcast prospecting, which turned out to be a miserable failure. When I started talking to people whom I knew, whom I already had personal credibility with, people started offering me money. OPM is a tremendous resource that can open all kinds of opportunities, so I encourage entrepreneurs to cultivate relationships that open doors to OPM. But I would also counsel people to not get intoxicated with it. It is someone else's money — so they should treat it better than their own.

When going to your OPM source to sell them on your idea, I found that personal credibility with them counted a lot. Second was my track record. I had already demonstrated that I had done this type of business before and was successful with it. In my case, I was not asking them to take a chance on a brand new idea that had not been tested, which made a big difference.

You may be hesitant to use OPM, but I say do it; get started. I cannot emphasize this enough: Using OPM was the one key critical success factor for my business. Without it, I would never have even gotten started. When using OPM, I would caution you to make sure you have set aside enough cash reserve or working capital, though. That was my biggest concern when I started, because without it, it is a sure way to get into trouble.

CASE STUDY: THE CASH FLOW MERCENARY

Once I began using private investor money, my concern became the safety and security of my investors' funds. I make my payments to them a couple of days early. Once one deal goes bad with a private investor, word will spread, and that source will disappear. It is nearly impossible to get a second chance, so treat private investors like gold. If there is ever the potential for a loss, I would rather it  be me who takes it than to leave my investor holding the bag. It is important to foster goodwill immediately with an investor. No matter how well I know someone, once they decide to invest in me, and money is changing hands, I know they are thinking about the worst-case scenario: I am not going to pay. So, the first payment is critical to cementing the relationship and putting them at ease. When I make my first payment to a private investor, if they are local, I deliver the check — in person — a couple of days before it is due. And I take a moderate-sized fruit basket as a gift. That generates additional investor leads for me, but it also helps overcome any buyer's remorse that may have set in because everyone in the office is blown away by having the check delivered early, and with a gift. I recommend that after that initial payment, pay your payments a day or two early every month, if possible.

When working with an investor, be sure to provide them with all the information they need in order to make a decision — but not too much information, because a confused mind always says no. It is important that the entrepreneur take cues from the investor about how much they need to know, and understand that the investor usually knows far less about the business than the entrepreneur does. However, the last thing you want is for them to feel misled, even if you live up to the terms of the agreement, so make sure you are not giving them less information than is necessary for them to make a decision. And when you talk business, make sure it is all business, even when they are your friend.

To be blunt, OPM put me on a fast track different from the one I had planned on in my automotive career: the one to financial security and independence. I cannot overstate the impact that OPM has had on my business. It is singularly responsible for me building a $2 million real estate portfolio consisting of 11 single-family houses and a 20-unit apartment building, and it will help me acquire the nine additional houses that I am in the process of buying.

Chapter 11:

Real Estate Investment with OPM

Benefits of Real Estate Investment

Many wealthy people got that way through real estate investment. Real estate is a direction a good number of investors take when it comes to building their wealth by building a portfolio of properties to either rent or sell. Because of the numbers associated with a property — such as the value, the surrounding real estate market, and the flexibility in the length of time you can hold or release a property — real estate is a popular way to use OPM. When it comes to convincing an investor to part with his or her money to invest with you, real estate offers a more tangible product than a business idea might.

> **Investors' Insight:**
> Real estate can be a gold mine, but it can also be a fool's gold mine if you are not careful with how you invest in it. While it can be an excellent vehicle for making money, it is not something to jump into without having done your research. There is more involved than driving past a "For Sale" sign and making an offer.

Real estate provides flexibility as an investment because of the many options that can be done with the property. Because of this, the terms upon which you borrow OPM from an investor can be just as flexible, leaving you the freedom to vary it with each deal. When you invest in real estate, having OPM as a source enables you to act quickly when it comes to excellent deals you come across. And, every deal you make can be different, depending on what you want to do with the property. Typically, people who invest in real estate can do one or a combination of the following:

- **Flip**: A property is purchased, fixed up, and quickly placed back on the market for a higher sale price than originally purchased.

- **Rent:** A property is purchased with the intent of holding on to it, allowing it to grow in value over a longer term, thereby creating a source of equity that can be tapped. The mortgage is paid by renters to cover the monthly expense while this nest egg is nurtured. If market conditions are favorable, such as a rising demand for rental properties that raises area rental fees, you can potentially secure additional cash flow if you are able to charge above the amount of your monthly mortgage. Someone else's money is essentially building your wealth for you, though you are ultimately responsible for the mortgage note.

- **Develop:** A piece of land is purchased with the intention of improving on it by building a residential or commercial structure.

You are not constrained by investing in only one type of real estate. You may want to specialize in one for the sake of convenience or to streamline your research, but nothing precludes you from purchasing a single-family home and a multi-family unit. Your interests could also venture over into the commercial side by purchasing buildings and leasing the space to other companies.

> $ *Investors' Insight:*
> Talk to everyone you come across in your community about your interest in real estate. Some of the best deals to be found will be word-of-mouth, simply from striking up a conversation. Also, have business cards to hand out. You may be surprised by a call in the future from someone you met casually months ago.

What to Look For

When evaluating a property, there are a couple of key factors to look for. First, look at what value you can add to it in order to make a profit. Buying real estate for investment purposes is not the same as when you are shopping for your primary home. It may not be the type of property where you would ever consider living, but that does not mean no one else will see it that way — especially if you improve upon it. You will also not want to become emotionally attached to any of the properties you are sifting through; instead, you will want to fall for the numbers that work in your favor. You are looking at the structure and what upgrades you can make to it so that it is attractive to another buyer, and you can sell it for more than for what you purchased it or rent it for more money. Your eye will need to be trained to look past a property that is not pretty on the outside but is solid beneath. Often, cleaning up the landscaping, making a few minor repairs, and repainting the exterior can create a significant improvement in a property's curb appeal and overall value.

One of the most important details to look for when evaluating property is whether there is a motivated seller behind it, as these are where you tend to find the most profitable deals. The two do not necessarily go hand-in-hand, though. The seller may be motivated, but the profit you want is not in the deal. Or, the seller is not motivated while you can see big dollar signs in the deal — if only they would see things your way. Some typical properties that can have motivated sellers behind them include:

1. **Foreclosure properties:** Due to job loss, illness, and even mismanagement of finances, there are many people who are in a situation where they are going to lose their home. They would like to prevent their credit from being ruined for potentially seven to 10 years, which is the standard amount of time that a foreclosure specifically will show up on your credit report, usually a much greater debt than one incurred and unpaid on a credit card. This negative reporting would prevent them from getting any kind of a loan until after that time period, which makes a lot of people feel motivated to avoid the situation in the first place.

2. **Divorces:** The property is the final link in the soon-to-be-released marital arrangement, and many people just want out as quickly and painlessly as possible while still receiving their share of any profit. The scenario could be that one party gets the house in the divorce agreement but is unable to keep up the mortgage on his or her own, or the property holds too many memories that the party does not want to revisit constantly. He or she is looking for that fresh start.

3. **Inherited property:** When a death occurs in the family and a property is passed to the heirs, many are not pre pared for the financial responsibility of suddenly having to take on a mortgage, the taxes, or the upkeep associated with the property. These parties will be looking to cash out as quickly as possible to relieve themselves of the responsibility in owning another property.

4. **Rentals:** Some landlords want out of their rental properties for a range of reasons, such as the burden of keeping the property maintained, the responsibility of continually finding tenants, or bad experiences with tenants who did not take care of the property. Or, they are simply ready to access the equity.

5. **Relocations:** Through job transfers, illness, or retirement, these owners will be motivated to move their properties quickly so the owners can get on with their life or finalize their arrangements.

Some of these properties are not necessarily found in the multiple listing service (MLS), which is the main database where real estate agents go to find properties that are available for sale. This means you will have to do some scouting. Obviously, it is easier to have the leads come to you rather than your having to spend time and effort hunting for them. You will want to network with people in the areas you are looking to invest in, letting people know you are interested in buying properties from motivated sellers and advertising the same message through various media.

When you do scout for properties, there are physical signs to look for that may hold promise as having a motivated seller hidden behind them:

1. **Homes for rent:** Just as above, when you see a rental sign, take note and contact them. Behind that rental sign may be an owner who has been toying with the idea of just selling and moving on — and it may be your phone call that prompts their decision.

2. **For sale by owner (FSBO):** Owners who are trying to sell their property on their own have a variety of reasons for skipping over the option of having an agent do it for them. Some have very little equity to play with and do not want to pay a real estate agent's commission on the sale; others want to maximize every cent of the profit. Eventually, they may weary of this slower process and want to just be rid of the property and will be willing to negotiate if they feel they will be treated in a manner they deem to be fair and equitable.

3. **Basic, low-end homes:** You do not want the most expensive property in a neighborhood because it does not leave much in the way of wiggle room when it comes to selling and getting the maximum amount of profit out of the deal. In the real estate market, the homes that sit the longest without a contract are usually the ones that are the most expensive properties in the neighborhood or have had a lot of customized upgrades done that suit the seller but are not necessarily beneficial when it comes to resale. Large homes in particular cost more to purchase, heat, and maintain, and these are the types of factors you will want to consider in how quickly you can move a property. Buyers may fall in love with a property, but they still have to do the math as to how they will afford it, so you do not want to be the highest price in the neighborhood. Also, a

home that has had a lot of customization may leave buyers wondering how their things will fit in. A basic, low-end home serves as an empty canvas rather than a source of confusion or cost-concern.

4. **Areas in transition:** Keep an eye on local happenings in your community. If there is a new enterprise being built or an influx of people expected due to jobs being established in the region to support a new industry, then homes that are situated close by have the potential of going up in value. Also, areas that are going through a period of revitalization and gentrification tend to see a bump in home values as a result.

5. **Run-down homes:** Due to illness, aging, or financial hardship, there are people who just cannot manage to keep up their homes any longer. They know that every problem not attended to further degrades their own investment and how much profit they can get from the sale, and they would like to get what they can while they still can.

Use A Marketing Approach to Purchase Real Estate

The best way to locate properties is through a combination of marketing efforts. One of the simplest ways is to knock on the door of a property that has a "For Sale" or "For Rent" sign in front of it. You can ask the source directly for a little history on the property and find out what it is they are trying to accomplish. Are they in financial trouble and need to move quickly? Is the house being sold due to a job loss, divorce, or death in the family? This is an aggressive approach, but you can quickly learn a lot from a quick conversation involving a few key questions that help you zoom in on the motivation behind the sign.

Another strategy to use is direct mail — sending either letters or postcards — offering to purchase properties. This is a slower approach, as direct mail has a low response rate. It does well if you look at it as part of your larger marketing effort. It will serve to help build name recognition — seven is the average number of times someone has to see a name in advertising before it sticks. Some recipients of your direct mail may hang on to it because they have been considering a move, or they know they may soon be in a situation, such as job loss, where they are forced to make a decision as to whether they will be able to hold on to their home, and they are gathering information. Again, this is a slower process, but you are building your portfolio. Some of those leads may come now, and some may not show up until further out on the calendar.

You have probably seen the plastic signs on the side of the road that say, "We buy houses." These signs can offer a great rate of return for the amount of work involved. Order enough signs to allow for a solid span of marketing time based on the research you did for the marketing portion of your business plan. Once you receive the signs, you will need to go to a hardware store to purchase wooden stakes and one-inch roofing nails. Nail your signs to the wooden stakes using two nails for each sign, putting the sign a few inches below the top of the stake, so that you will not smash the top of the sign while hammering the stake into the ground. After your signs are ready to go, you need to have a campaign ready that provides you a schedule for putting them up. You want to be consistent about placing them up, and you also want to make sure to place them in areas where there is a high volume of traffic. Before posting any signs, you will want to check with the local county office to see if there are any sign restrictions you should follow. This can include where you are allowed to place signs, what streets you can place them on, time limits, and removal. Failure to comply with those restrictions could result in fines. Those penalties can quickly add up, cutting into the profits of your efforts.

Work the Numbers

When you find a property that you think has good investment potential, you will want to do the math to see if the investment makes sense from a financial perspective. Only you know how much you want to make out of a real estate deal. Your short- and long-term goals, and the amount of investment needed to get the property in selling condition, are factors to take into consideration that will influence your numbers.

Here is a simple formula to calculate the approximate potential value of the property so you can estimate how much you can list it for on the market once you have done some upgrades:

Price + Fix-Up Cost = After Rehab Value (ARV)

Next, you will do a competitive market analysis of the market surrounding the area where the property is located and determine what the range is for properties being sold. Newspapers for an area will run listings for recently sold properties; this provides a snapshot in time, as market values can fluctuate — even in good markets. Again, a good rule of thumb is to make sure you are not intending to do so many upgrades on the property that you end up making no profit on your investment. Then, you would have to price the property a lot higher to earn back the money you have put into it, but it is now priced at the high-end of its surrounding location. Include in your competitive market analysis what properties are currently available and what they are being priced for, so you can evaluate the amount of investment to put into renovations and still secure a profit. Your goal is to maximize your return on investment while minimizing your risk.

In order to determine the costs involved to fix up the property, you will need a contractor to give you an estimated dollar amount for those upgrades. Once you know how much it will cost to fix up and the profit you are looking to earn on the investment, you will have a number to put forth as an offer to the seller.

Negotiating the Real Estate Deal

Everything is negotiable, including property prices. Most people who are selling or buying a property understand they will have to give some concessions so that all parties are satisfied with the transaction. The conditions of the market can, in large part, dictate who goes into the deal with the upper hand. At the height of the real estate buying and selling frenzy that occurred when housing values started increasing, hitting a peak around 2005, sellers were treated to offers being thrown at them, with buyers sometimes trying to outbid one another in an effort to secure a coveted property. Currently, the market is more favorable to the buyer: With a glut of properties from which to choose, buyers have the option of being more demanding about what they want and the price they want to pay for it. For either scenario, there will be a deal that needs to be negotiated before a property can be moved off the market.

When you are preparing to negotiate the deal, whether it is with the home owner, a real estate agent, or a bank, know what you want out of the deal, what you would be willing to negotiable and, most definitely, what is non-negotiable. Have a plan and stick to it, and know when to walk away. Any investment you do is going to rely a good deal on your gut feeling about its favorable prospects coupled with solid research — especially the more experienced you become in making investments, as you learn first-hand how your research and instincts match up.

Negotiating real estate deals usually begins with the investor making a formal offer to the seller in writing, just as any other buyer would do. Prior to the offer, you may have already had several conversations with the seller and have an idea of what they are looking for in the deal, making it easier to craft the offer rather than flying blindly into it, unsure of what to expect. The written offer should cover all aspects of how you envision the deal proceeding, taking into account the information gathered in these conversations and your own research into the property's market value and addressing any concerns by presenting your solutions. The offer should contain a contingency clause that allows for the completion of a professional inspection to be done of the property for any issues not readily apparent by the investor's inspection. This protects you and helps minimize the risk of the investment. There is nothing worse than taking on a property that you estimate will bring you a certain return on your investment, only to see that return swallowed up by costly repairs that you did not factor into the equation. Upon completion of this inspection, if the unexpected does occur, you can decide how to proceed: Either renegotiate the deal to make financial allowance for the findings, or withdraw your offer and move on to another investment property.

A word of caution: Make sure you check to see if there are any title problems. An unclear title can cause you headaches and loss of profit potential when it comes time for you to sell. The land records office in the county where the property is located is where you will find the title record. Title insurance can be taken out to protect against any surprises that may come with a title that has problems attached to it, such as unpaid property taxes — and any potential financial loss you would incur. One problem could be the government, utilities, or companies that have a lien against the property, and your claim to the title falls behind theirs. Another problem could be that the person selling you the home has no authority to do so.

What To Do With Real Estate

At the beginning of the chapter, there was a quick overview of the different options available to the investor who is interested in acquiring real estate as a means to build wealth. The following offers a more in-depth look at those options.

Flipping properties

A property that is bought low and sold high is the ideal situation for an investor to have. Investors purchase the property and stick to a timeline that allows for renovations and upgrades to be done as quickly as possible so that the property is not held for long — with its mortgage and utility meter running. For a flip

investment, the investor weighs the number of upgrades to pour into the property with an eye on details — such as pricing it so it will sell as soon as possible once placed on the market, why the property has now appreciated in value, and why the property is being offered at a higher price than what it was purchased for. When the market began its downturn around 2006, many investors were left holding properties for longer than they had budgeted for. Investors took a hit to their profit expectations and, in some cases, lost money or the property altogether to foreclosure. Investors who look at doing a flip in slow market conditions need to adjust their profit expectations and timelines accordingly to allow for a property that may sit longer and return less on the initial investment. Flipping properties has been an attractive option from the standpoint of a quick return on investment with a sometimes substantial profit earned for the outlay of time and expenditure. But when the market is offering more homes for sale than there are buyers for them, you may want to reevaluate the flipping-properties portion of your real estate investment plan and look at it as a long-term investment rather than fast cash.

Besides the fact that market conditions can do their own flip, another negative side of flipping properties is that you are constantly prowling to locate new properties to turn over. And rather than having a steady income, it is a one-time chunk of cash, and sometimes not the amount that you were counting on. In addition, with tight timelines to complete renovations and a limited budget set forth, there is generally not much room for miscues, contractors and sub-contractors who do not show up to complete a job when expected — creating a domino effect for other contractors who need the first part of the plan completed — or nasty surprises revealed during the renovation process. Flipping homes can be a delicate balancing act and takes patience, diplomacy, and the ability to be your own project manager.

Buying and holding

If your goal is to have a passive income rolling in, then you will need to have a stable of properties that you hold onto, lumping them together and treating them as a long-term investment. This gives the properties time to accrue equity, and you can sell them as needed or continue to enjoy the influx of passive income. If you can use the profits from the sale of some of the properties to pay off the loans on the others, you will have just the recurring income to collect and no more loan payments, satisfying the repayment portion of using OPM and now collecting the financial rewards you went into this for in the first place. This is the ideal to reach for when buying and holding, as it rewards your patience in not going for the "get rich quick" investment strategy — one we are not likely to see again in our lifetimes.

Develop real estate

Whether for residential or commercial purposes, there is a need somewhere for someone to take land and develop it for use. Industries spring up in an area, and there is a need for housing for the workers who will be drawn there. When that housing development goes up, that area will now have a need for office and retail space so those residents have some place to do business and shop. There are also commercial buildings that need to be re-purposed for other uses. Where there is a need, it may be your company that fills it. Keep your eyes — and your options — open. If developing land is something that appeals to you, it is a good idea to start small and build so you can form your experience, confidence, and credibility before moving to even bigger projects. Or, if your vision is big enough, focus on that business plan and how you are going to make it happen. Either way, you will need to convince investors to provide you with the money to launch this venture. This highlights a recurring theme throughout this book: The necessity of a solid business plan that shows you have done your research — and shows a return on investment to your OPM providers.

Financing Options

The buyer

Seller financing can put somebody in a property with zero down. This is actually the real power behind what is called seller carry-back financing, as in the case of a "For Sale By Owner" (FSBO). There is a giant market for FSBO properties in the residential market as well as commercial. Every major city in the United States has a free FSBO magazine at supermarkets and convenience stores, as well as an online version. The situation at the moment with real estate has left many agents with an overabundance of properties that they are unable to sell or finance. Currently, approximately 15 percent of all properties in both Texas and California are being sold using this method, and other states have already begun to follow their example.

Of the 15 percent of these FSBO real estate deals, approximately 12 percent are being set up through seller carry-back financing. Seller carry-back is very simple: The seller sells a property for which the buyer cannot qualify for a loan. There are many reasons that a buyer may not be qualified, beyond bad credit or bankruptcy. Perhaps they are self-employed or have just gotten divorced. Sometimes even doctors can get turned down for a loan because of their self-employment status. The point is, there are a lot of qualified buyers who are unable to purchase a property, and if you can reach these people, you are going to be ahead as far as real estate goes.

Any sale can potentially be made, as long as you have a willing seller and a willing buyer who can agree on a price for the value of the property. There are no bank approvals to speak of — just two people getting together and deciding what they want to do. It will not cost you a single dime, and it is considered OPM because the seller is willing to carry back the loan on the property. You can offer the seller a better interest rate to encourage them to make the deal with you.

The seller

What can you do as a seller to sell your home when every third house along a neighborhood has a "For Sale" sign? What attracts a buyer to stop at one house and not the house next door that looks just like it? The answer to this question is the "For Sale By Owner" sign. The National Association of Realtors (**www.realtor.com**) claims that 86 percent of all home buyers go to the Internet before they ever visit the office of a real estate agent. This is an opportunity for private sellers when they are trying to sell a property. Keep in mind that this person will also not be paying a 4 to 6 percent fee to a real estate agent. Their investment is simply placing a sign out in their yard and a few dollars to feature their property online.

A seller can basically do everything on his or her own that a real estate agent can do to sell a home. In addition, the seller has the advantage of negotiating the zero-down payment because they can set up the financial deal in any way they see fit and that makes financial sense to them. There is no rule that says you have to go to a bank to buy a home. If, as the seller, you are willing to forgo the step of waiting for your buyer to obtain a loan by offering seller financing, you will increase your chances of finding a buyer. Carrying a loan makes sense in many other aspects beyond making a quick sale. From a tax standpoint, an installment loan sale will allow the seller to pay much less in taxes over the course of the note than the traditional means of a buyer mortgage or loan.

It is a win-win for both the buyer and the seller. The buyer gets what they want, which is a zero-down payment. The seller gets what they want, which is their asking price and a note secured by the property. If the note fails, they can always get the property back. Sellers can make it very simple to protect themselves from the occurrence of a failed note by doing a "deed in lieu of foreclosure." This deed can be drawn up at the time of the sale of the property. It says that if a payment is missed by more than 30 days, the deal is foreclosed by mutual consent. In the situation of a failed note, there is no need for a court case; the seller will get their property back, and they can then sell it again. There is nothing lost, while several payments have been gained.

Brokers are bar busters

Brokers are notorious for raising the bar as high as they can to get your business, then slowly lowering it in order to get it sold. A broker's main concern is to get you to sign a deal. Some of them will tell you anything that you want to hear in order to sell your home. The problem here is that they raise the expectations of their clients so much that when they inevitably have to start lowering the cost, it can bring out hard feelings on the part of the seller. They feel as if they are losing money when, in fact, they are usually selling for the worth of their home for the market they are in.

People form an emotional attachment to their own property, making it a challenge for them to evaluate the property from the standpoint of what the market will bear. You should always get a proper appraisal before selling or buying any property, as it is a neutral evaluation based on the reality of the existing real estate market.

Financing

Real estate has many creative ways of being financed beyond the traditional bank-financed method and through the use of OPM, different from financing other types of business ventures. There are a few options for acquiring real estate, including wholesaling and lease options, and subject to — all of which do not require your holding a mortgage.

- **Wholesaling:** Wholesaling is assigning a contract to another investor for an assignment fee. For example, when you get a property under contract for $50,000 but do not want to close on it yourself, you assign the contract to another investor for a $5,000 assignment fee and make a quick $5,000.

- **Lease options:** Lease options are leasing the property with an option to purchase at some point. For example, John Doe, the seller, has a house he is renting out for $1,000 a month. You tell him you will rent the house for 10 years at

$1,000 a month, and that you will buy it for $150,000. Once this first step is accomplished, you turn around and sublet the house to a tenant. You give them a two-year lease with option to buy and rent the property for $1,200 a month, selling it for $175,000. Your profit will, of course, become the difference.

- **Subject to:** This option is when you purchase a property "subject to" the seller's existing mortgage. In simpler terms, you are buying someone's house and taking over their monthly mortgage payments. Because you are not getting a loan in your own name, you are able to own an unlimited number of properties, which will be to your advantage because you will not be bogged down in debt as you continue to acquire properties.

There are other financing options to investigate, as well. The following you will recognize to be the general sources of OPM that can be accessed for any business deal, including real estate:

- **Commercial banks:** They offer traditional mortgage products and stringent guidelines that include have excellent credit. Commercial loans can also take longer to get than some other sources of money. However, it is an option, and one to consider for your needs.

- **Private lenders/investor groups:** A variety of investors who are non-traditional, each with their own terms and conditions to loans.

- **Angel investors:** Wealthy individuals or a network of wealthy individuals who have the funds to invest in deals that interest them.

- **Venture capitalists:** They consider investing in businesses to be their profession.

- **Friends and family:** You may already know someone who has money languishing in a savings account and is looking for the opportunity to earn a bigger return on their money. They may be interested in earning it through investing with you on a real estate deal.

- **Grants:** Grants that you can apply for depending on whom your project is going to help. For example, if you develop a property for seniors or special-needs individuals, there may be programs available to help. Grants are also available to promote job creation and training, to develop a location, and to help the disadvantaged. A government program called Small Business Innovative Research (**www. sbir.gov**) promotes ideas that will help people or contribute to quality of life, offering grants to develop these ideas. Subsidies from the government encourage projects considered to be in the public interest. Many properties could be revitalized to fulfill the parameters of a public-interest project, which, depending on the property, makes looking at grants an attractive source for real estate investing.

The following financing options are specific to just real estate transactions:

- **Assumption of mortgage:** All loans are assumable one year after being taken out, meaning an investor can take over the existing loan and purchase the property at a discount. The investor then becomes responsible for the loan payments. An assumption is a good option for an investor if the interest rate on the existing loan is better than the prevailing rates, thereby saving the investor money that would otherwise be paid out in interest. Research to see how old the loan is, the balance on the loan, and what type of loan it is.

- **Sale and lease-back**: This is similar to what was described as a source of money for equipment as a general financing option. You can do the same with real estate: A seller relinquishes title, then leases back (rents) the property. This can help some homeowners avoid foreclosure and provide them the opportunity to get their financial portfolio together while remaining in the home, and possibly buy back the property after a certain term.

- **HELOC:** If you have an existing property that has equity, you can apply for a home equity line of credit (HELOC) to use for the purchase of another. The HELOC allows you to obtain a line of credit up to a percentage of the value of your current property. Some investors saw their lines of credit slashed as home values went into decline starting around 2006.

- **Bridge (interim) loan:** These loans use less strict rules of refinancing than the basic loan. A bridge loan can be done for a short term, such as a month, while the next phase of the investor's plan is being worked on, such as an immediate sale to another buyer.

- **REIT:** Real estate investment trusts (REIT) are groups of investors who pool their funds to invest in the purchasing and managing of properties. You can invest in real estate with a group without direct ownership of the property. The disadvantage is you do not own property outright and therefore are subject to the goals of the collective group, rather than your own.

- **Hard money lenders:** These are investors who loan money for the purpose of rehabbing properties to increase the value and resell at a profit.

- **Conduit loans:** Investor money is pooled, typically for commercial real estate deals, and these are generally favorable in regard to interest rates, terms, and conditions for the borrower.

CASE STUDY: THE FOSSIL CARTEL

The Fossil Cartel
Pioneer Place #1440
340 SW Morrison
Portland, OR 97204
www.fossilcartel.com
susan@fossilcartel.com
Phone: (503) 228-6998
Susan Landa — Owner

I do not remember when I first heard about OPM. I thought it was common knowledge. What I do know is that my dreams had been on hold for probably about a year before I went for it.

OPM helped me buy my house when I only had $2,000 to my name and no job — I was a self-employed crafter. Needless to say, I would not have been able to get a conventional mortgage. What happened was that a woman (she was the mother of a friend) bought a house so that I could buy it from her on a private contract. The second time I used OPM, it helped me start my business, which hit 20 years in August 2009. The business lender was a friend of my first husband. Also, the equity in my house allowed me to borrow more money for my business, so that initial OPM deal went a long way.

If you are interested in obtaining OPM, I would advise that you make sure the source can afford to gamble on you. OPM should be viewed even more seriously than money from an institution because it is coming from an individual.

I would caution you to be careful when choosing your investors. The OPM source for my business seemed like he wanted to "keep me in my place" and have me do the "woman work" — like bookkeeping and paperwork. He thought my husband was the real business person. It turned out otherwise, and he had to deal with it. The original arrangement set up between him and my first husband fell through because my husband reneged on his word. But I took responsibility and made sure the friend got his money back.

Make sure the deal is very clear to begin with, and follow through. Also make sure in advance that the investor understands their relationship to the business and what their role would be, if any. Report on the status of the business once a quarter. Depending on the investor, ask for feedback so they can feel involved and respected.

As an entrepreneur first entering the OPM waters, what you can expect going in totally depends on the type of OPM source you are using. If you are talking about angel money, the hoops one has to jump through are numerous. You have

CASE STUDY: THE FOSSIL CARTEL

to have a complete business plan, executive summary, elevator pitch, proven market/product, a visual presentation, due diligence, lawyers to draw up stock arrangements, and much more. The list of requirements is quite extensive. If it is a friend or relative, it depends on your relationship to them. It can really be all over the board.

When it came to securing OPM, I have to credit my ex-husband's charm and persuasiveness that convinced his friend to invest. Originally they were going to be in business together as wholesalers. It morphed into my ex and I retailing the merchandise, which became our business. My ex is a phenomenal "talker." He can talk almost anyone into anything. I think that is truly what made the difference in gaining access to the OPM for the business.

Chapter 12:

Other Uses of OPM

Pay Off Debts

Debt is one of the major killers of any start-up business venture. There is only so much debt that a business can collect before that debt will start to eat the business alive from the inside out. Part of the intent of this book is to teach you to use OPM to your benefit so that you will have access to money that may not be available to you through the use of some of the more conventional sources of OPM. But, eventually, you will more than likely come to a wall in your financial acquisitions and find yourself having to turn to the conventional means of OPM, such as credit cards and commercial banks. These leave a nagging monthly payment that only seems to grow larger the further you go into debt. This is why you may need to obtain a loan through one of the means we have discussed that involves a high interest rate. If you do go this route, continue to look for a source of OPM that will offer a trade in resources or equity, so you can limit the amount of debt that you are accruing on your balance sheet.

It is essential to avoid increasing a debt that you are unable to pay to begin with; it is growing in fines and fees, and is ruining your credit score. Debt is one of the biggest problems in the United States right now, and it is because credit has been all too readily available. Usually the easiest credit to get might not be in your best interest because of the high rates and multiple fees. If you do have to use a high-interest loan, focus on replacing that debt with a more desirable OPM investment plan as soon as possible. It may sound strange to hear, but some debt is better than other types, and OPM debt may be the salvation you will need to keep your business out of trouble if it is beginning to succumb to high-interest credit debt that you may be carrying, regardless of the source. Always look for the better deal and evaluate the cost of the money you are borrowing, whether it be from a venture capitalist, a family member, or a commercial bank.

$ Investors' Insight:
Securing OPM does not mean you are permanently finished with evaluating everything to do with that money. What may have been a good deal when you were a fledgling business may now prove to be an anchor, so it literally pays to keep your options open as much as contract terms and the markets allow.

The other end of the spectrum is what we discussed in regard to managing your OPM. If you find you are doing better than you had originally projected on your business plan, it may make sense to leverage that positive outcome, secure better debt, and pay off excess debt that has a high interest rate attached to it.

Invest in Paper Assets

Part of your business strategy may include investments on behalf of the business. There are investors who prefer to take a passive role: They supply the money based on an agreement of a certain return on their investment that they feel comfortable with, and you do the work of creating that ROI. Your business plan may include a wide range of avenues for creating wealth, some of which will be used to sustain the business or serve as a reserve to be drawn on for expansion opportunities. It makes little sense to have money on hand that languishes in a savings account, earning very little. Your plan may include investing in some of the following assets that are not tangible but can be vehicles of financial growth that can be drawn on and used at a future date.

Bonds

Considered a security, bonds are generally a fairly slow and safe method for financial gain. It does not offer the big money potential of stocks, but its safety margin is built into the reduction of risk for loss of the investment. A bondholder is thought of as a lender to the issuer with a promise to be paid back within a defined term. The federal government, state governments, and large companies usually offer bonds. This gives them money to operate or initiate projects. The purchaser of the bond is paid back once the bond "matures," similar to a certificate of deposit coming due — only they tend to be over a longer timeframe, such as ten years or more, depending on what is being issued to investors. This long-term investment is also a risk, should inflation go up and the value of the dollar drop. If this happens, your money is stuck in that bond for its term. Types of bonds include:

- **U.S. government bonds**: Known as Treasury bonds, these bonds have maturity periods that vary between ten and 30 years.

- **Municipal bonds**: State and local governments will issue bonds so they can complete civic projects, such as building roads. The federal government has made them attractive by making their interest payments exempt from federal taxes.

- **Corporate bonds**: Issued by larger companies with terms that can range from one year on up. The longer the term, the greater the risk, as a company could go bankrupt before the bond reaches its maturity date.

- **Savings bonds**: These can be picked up at a bank, being purchased for exactly half the value of the bond's worth. They can be cashed in as needed or allowed to earn interest for up to 30 years.

Stocks

Also considered a security, the holder of stock owns a part of that business and actually has a share of equity at stake. However, there is no promise of a certain return at any given point in time. Instead, the stockholder may have to wait indefinitely to see a positive return in money, and he or she may end up losing some of it in the process. Stocks are generally known to be riskier, but more risk translates to greater potential gain. Which paper asset is the most appropriate choice for you depends on how much money you can stand to lose.

Investment in stocks with OPM is almost never recommended due to the unpredictable nature. The problem with stocks is that no matter how good you may be — or think you are — there will come a time when your luck will run out, and that could be the point where you lose everything. If you want to play in

stocks, make sure to leave yourself room to play without losing everything. Everyone who plays in the stock market eventually loses — whether it is a small fraction or the entire lot — because the stock market runs in cyclical ups and downs; how much you lose will be up to you. Losing OPM in a stock investment is not a smart business practice because you can cut off your access to other sources of OPM if it looks like you have previously gambled away funds. It would be similar to asking an investor to give you money to go to Las Vegas and hit the casinos, promising them a huge return on their investment.

On the safe side of things are the long-term equity anticipation securities (known as LEAPS) that allow an investor to establish a conservative position with a growing company for a period of up to three years without having to make an outright stock purchase. These offer a huge growth potential with minimal risk, as the risk is hedged somewhat in the event of a loss. So while stocks are a risky business, there are those who can take advantage and maneuver around such risk to create a sizable profit.

Hedge funds

A hedge fund is open to a limited number of wealthy and professional investors. The limitation allows them to sidestep investment regulations that are in place for larger investment groups, such as regular investment funds. They pay a performance fee to an investment manager who manages on their behalf a broad range of aggressive investments designed to maximize the return on investment.

While hedge funds can be a somewhat risky proposition, some investors believe that you can play these risky stocks to maximize your gains, while at the same time minimize your losses. Timothy Sykes, Season 1 star of the MOJO reality TV show *Wall Street Warriors* and author of *An American Hedge Fund*, is one such believer. Sykes took $12,415, invested in the stock market while in college, and turned it into $1.65 million before starting his own hedge fund company. When he did it, the market was at a prime point, and he did it using penny stocks, which are low-priced stocks. While he was sometimes dealing in risky stocks to maximize his gains, he played them safely to minimize his losses, such as putting in stop losses that automatically sold the stock if they dropped more than 8 percent.

When people hear about hedge funds, it is usually through their failure rather than success. This is not to say that hedge funds are not without risk, but you can minimize this further by investing in funds of funds (FOFs). An FOF is like a mutual fund in that they are grouped together into several different funds. This minimizes the risk of investing in just one and having it collapse. Something else to consider is that above mutual fund investments, FOF allow the investor to short sale and bet against the market, which would have come in handy during the 2008-2009 stock market drought.

Index funds

Not every stock has high-risk, though. One of the safest investments you could possibly make is with index funds. Index funds are based on purchasing securities, which are an investment contract with a value attached to it offering an interest in something, and are chosen by computer models, meaning there is no active investment manager of the fund. These investments follow and try to mimic the movements of financial indices such as the Dow Jones and Standard & Poor's 500 (S&P 500). Index funds are not as exciting as many of the high-risk stocks waiting to make someone wealthy beyond their imagination, or even poorer than they could have ever imagined possible. Index funds are similar to waiting for a pot of water to boil: They require patience as they take time to build up steam.

CASE STUDY: MICHAEL EDESESS

Investment Industry Insider
http://medesess.com
Michael Edesess — Investment insider and author of
The Big Investment Lie

Where most investments create their greatest fortunes is through their investor. In other words, you may be wasting your money if you are currently using an investment manager to help with your investments.

The principles that I follow for safe investing are diversification, low cost, low tax, and avoiding investment manager fees. Every one of these principles will lead you to the same place. Index funds are low-cost, low tax, masters of diversification, and you can do them yourself. Of the various index funds available, I prefer Vanguard, in which I invest half my total money in their total market index fund.

As for hedge funds, they are mostly hype. Just as there is anecdotal evidence that some people who go to Las Vegas will get rich, there is, of course, anecdotal evidence of some hedge funds doing well — but in general, they do quite poorly. The people who claim that there is money to be made through hedge funds do not know what they are talking about. There are more than 10,000 hedge funds, and while some will do well some of the time, there is really no way to be able to predict which ones will. Hedge fund managers collect gigantic fees from their clients and investors. These investors on average do not do well at all. Every once in a while, the ones who take the greatest risks get a big payoff and further drive the lie.

In hedge funds, the perception is that if you are rich, you can get much richer more quickly than other people can because you have the privilege to be able to invest in hedge funds. In actuality, it is no privilege at all because they do worse than ordinary index funds. These are low-cost funds that buy the entire market. The average hedge fund does worse than that. When you are investing in a hedge fund and have to pay hedge-fund fees, you will have one-third to one-fourth as much money by the time you have retired, as you would have had if

CASE STUDY: MICHAEL EDESESS

you had invested in a very simple, low-cost index fund.

The fact is: If you use leverage and borrow to invest, then if your investments do well, you will do even better. If you borrow half of what you invest, then if your investment goes up 10 percent, your investment will go up 20 percent because you borrowed to invest twice as much. You still have to pay back with interest what you have borrowed, but still you wind up with maybe 15 percent, which is more than the 10 percent using all your own money.

The problem is when it goes down, you will lose more than twice as much. So you are always increasing your risk level when you borrow. It depends on how much risk you can stand to take. If you risk too much, you will be almost certain to go broke sooner or later. They say that the more risk you take, the more return you get, but it is not a necessary connection. If you take more risk, you can get more return if you get lucky, but you will do much worse if you get unlucky. There is an awful lot of happenstance because the return on investment depends on future events, and unless you are some sort of a clairvoyant and can see in the future better than anybody else, it is just a matter of luck.

As you gain entrance into the investment market of OPM, be forewarned that the managers make much of the investor profits made through OPM; they make their money from fees. People think that fees charged by professional investment managers and advisors are small, or at least justifiable. They are neither. Annual revenues of the professional investment advice and management industries total about $500 billion. All of this comes directly out of investors' wealth, usually charged as a percentage of investment assets. In this case, as the investor, using OPM to gain access to the advice of a professional investment manager may not be the best way to spend these hard-earned dollars.

Most of the investing public is deluded in believing that professional investment advisors and managers can do better than a simple market average. This belief is nourished by a plethora of ads run by the large financial institutions. But the evidence — and with good reason — overwhelmingly contradicts that notion. The fleet of professional investment advisors and managers performs no better in their investment picks than would the fleet of Los Angeles garbage truck drivers if they were to pick investments. This statement is supported by decades of evidence and dozens of carefully researched statistical studies. It is a well-known fact among academicians and many others, yet the advertising mill (and the fawning financial media mill) is able constantly to drown out the evidence.

CASE STUDY: MICHAEL EDESESS

I could say that getting into the investment field is a good way to make money. But it should be understood that the way you make that money is by charging very high fees to clients who do not realize that you are really not helping them earn any more on their investments. Anybody can actually receive the credentials to call themselves a financial planner or advisor; it just takes a few tests. We are by no means recommending the use of OPM for gain through these means as much as we are giving you insight so that you will carefully consider your options before hiring an investment manager. It is quite simple to calculate the potential of an investment manager. The standard rate for an investment-manager who recommends asset allocations is about 1 percent of the client's money they invested. This may not sound like much from an investor's point of view, but if you take 1 percent of, say, $3 million, the manager will make no less than $30,000 on that deal.

When I was with a New York firm, we were trying to recruit tax accountants, CPAs who were interested in becoming investment advisors. We were trying to do this because we would provide services to them, and they would pay us a percent in the assets that they advised on. So it was to expand our business as well as help them expand theirs. These were people who basically just did people's taxes. We met with one of them, and to give him an example of the possibilities, we asked him to give us an example of one of his clients. He said that he had a client with about $3 million dollars that he could invest. We told him that the routine was to recommend an asset allocation, you recommend some business, and you take a percent for doing that.

Later on in the evening, he realized that 1 percent of $3 million is $30,000. He said he had never been able to charge that guy more than $3,000 before. It is easy to sell people on becoming investment advisors because they charge a percent of somebody's total investments, and it makes it sound like they are not charging very much, but it is actually huge. The big investment lie with hedge funds is that every once in awhile, one does well. The classic example is this long-term capital management, the big hedge fund that failed in 1998. It had three or four years of spectacular returns, and then it lost everything within the next year. They were taking a lot of risk and thought they were so smart, but they were not.

Not to say that the hedge fund managers think that they are just milking their clients. They think that every time they happen to get lucky and their funds go up, they are really smart. Then, the next year when everything goes down, they think they just ran into some bad luck — but they are still really "smart."

CASE STUDY: MICHAEL EDESESS

The other best way to make money with OPM is to let people think that you are doing something really smart for them. Most investment advisors do not really make people think that they are going to make a lot of money for them because they cannot really claim that. They have certain phrases that they use to suggest that.

If you went to an investment advisor and asked, "Why should I not just invest in a low-cost index fund?" they will give you all kinds of arguments why you should not do so, but they are all wrong. They will try to imply that you will earn more if you hire them than you would if you just invest in the entire stock market through an index fund. But they cannot actually say that you will earn more, because it is not true.

Conclusion

O PM can help you live the life you envision and build wealth while you are at it. Your efforts to achieve your financial goals also benefit others, like the investors who are also looking for opportunities just like you. The intention of this book was to show the possibilities of OPM and the ways it can be used; but behind every idea, you will find there is even greater depth — similar to the tip of an iceberg. There is a lot going on beneath the surface left to investigate in terms of details and expansion of your knowledge. Changes in the economy lead to ripple effects through markets, affecting how business is conducted. Consumer habits and lifestyles are always in a state of flux, requiring new ways and means of doing things. Whole books have been devoted to just one of these topics alone, and your education has only begun. But make no mistake: Your true education will be received in the *doing* that is necessary to bring your dreams to life.

And it is the action that you will have to initiate. If you find the thought of taking such a big leap of faith to be intimidating, know that you are not alone in your fear. Even seasoned entrepreneurs can feel jittery each time they start a new venture. It would take one cool and collected person to jump into the unknown with hardly a quiver of anxiety. Wherever you are starting from, it may feel like it is an insurmountable task to even know where to begin. But for your dreams to come alive, you have to start somewhere. You may have the perception that people who have built wealth are fundamentally different than you. But the only thing that separates you from them is that they have already taken the first step and have kept moving. Throughout this book, you have read case studies about people who are just like you, and the majority of them started right where you are: scared — yet *determined* to move past the fear and take the risk. You may be surprised to learn that fear is something that they each felt as they began their business ventures, and for many, that fear is still present. Only now, they use it as a chief motivator to stay on the track of success. Read their stories and absorb their words. Search for those common ties that you share. Hopefully, you will find in their experiences something that will inspire you to blaze your own trail on the path to a successful business launch.

By reading this book, you have already begun to move forward; so, start building. After you put this book down, it is up to you to decide where you will go and what you will do next. Maybe as you were reading, certain ideas resonated with you. If they struck you in some way, then pursue them. Remember: It is the dreams we are passionate about that have the likelihood of success because they do not let go of our imagination easily.

In addition, be sure to talk to business people in your family, in your community, and online. Ask them what they do, how they do it, and how they got started. You will find people are generally eager to share their experiences and knowledge with others, perhaps remembering that they were once where you are now — and others helped them with valuable advice. Read about what is going on in the world and in your own backyard. Create a plan of action that will move you forward on a dream that has been playing in the back of your mind. Take a step, then another. Learn, engage, explore, and keep moving forward until what was once a dream has become your waking reality. Keep a vigilant eye out for opportunities, and be open to them. And when they arrive, embrace and carry them through. Seek out OPM, and give a platform to those opportunities so they will benefit you and your investors.

You have begun your first step by purchasing and reading this book through to the end. Take that next step to build wealth. Remember to dream big, aim high, and by all means, have fun while you do it.

Resources

Federal Government Resource Web Sites

www.grants.gov

www.sba.gov

www.business.gov

www.womenbiz.gov

State Resource Web Sites

Alabama: **www.state.al.us**

Alaska: **www.state.ak.us**

Arizona: **www.state.az.us**

Arkansas: **www.state.ar.us**

California: **www.state.ca.us**

Colorado: **www.state.co.us**

Connecticut: **www.state.ct.us**

Delaware: **www.state.de.us**

District of Columbia: **www.state.dc.us**

Florida: **www.state.fl.us**

Georgia: **www.state.ga.us**

Hawaii: **www.state.hi.us**

Idaho: **www.state.id.us**

Illinois: **www.state.il.us**

Indiana: **www.state.in.us**

Iowa: **www.state.ia.us**

Kansas: **www.state.ks.us**

Kentucky: **www.state.ky.us**

Louisiana: **www.state.la.us**

Maine: **www.state.me.us**

Maryland: **www.state.md.us**

Massachusetts: **www.state.ma.us**

Michigan: **www.state.mi.us**

Minnesota: **www.state.mn.us**

Mississippi: **www.state.ms.us**

Missouri: **www.state.mo.us**

Montana: **www.state.mt.us**

Nebraska: **www.state.ne.us**

Nevada: **www.state.nv.us**

New Hampshire: **www.state.nh.us**

New Jersey: **www.state.nj.us**

New Mexico: **www.state.nm.us**

New York: **www.state.ny.us**

North Carolina: **www.state.nc.us**

North Dakota: **www.state.nd.us**

Ohio: **www.state.oh.us**

Oklahoma: **www.state.ok.us**

Oregon: **www.state.or.us**

Pennsylvania: **www.state.pa.us**

Puerto Rico: **www.state.pr.us**

Rhode Island: **www.state.ri.us**

South Carolina: **www.state.sc.us**

South Dakota: **www.state.sd.us**

Tennessee: **www.state.tn.us**

Texas: **www.state.tx.us**

Utah: **www.state.ut.us**

Vermont: **www.state.vt.us**

Virginia: **www.state.va.us**

Washington: **www.state.wa.us**

Wisconsin: **www.state.wi.us**

Wyoming: **www.state.wy.us**

Glossary

A

AMA: American Marketing Association; the largest marketing association in North America. It is a professional association for individuals and organizations involved in the practice, teaching, and study of marketing worldwide.

Amortization: Deduct the loss incurred by paying a premium from the interest (or gain) received from the bond.

Angel Investor: Individuals who are high-net-worth investors, looking for the highest return.

Assets: As an accounting or investment term, assets refer to owned items, such as cash, stock, equipment, and real estate.

B

Balance Sheet: Fluid financial statement used to look at a business's performance at a given point in time.

Bond: A bond is a contract representing the terms of borrowing and repayment for a debt.

C

Cash Flow Statement: Shows how much cash is needed to

run the business and when that cash is needed.

CDC: Certified development company; mortgage product that supports local community developments through commercial real estate.

CDs: Certificates of deposit; a time deposit with a fixed, specific term and usually a fixed interest rate.

Collateral Loan: Property acceptable as security for a loan or other obligation.

Commission: A fee or percentage allowed to a sales representative or an agent for services rendered.

Corporation: Most common form of business organization; chartered by a state and given many legal rights as an entity separate from its owners.

D

Diversification: Refers to the numbers and types of securities held; extends beyond the confines of a single type of investment.

Dividends: Payments made by corporations on earning as part of the profits and income are shared with investors.

E

EOL: Economic opportunity loans; loan for the low-income business owner who therefore may be experiencing more difficulty in securing financing, despite having a sound business idea. As long as one business partner is considered to be living below the poverty level (determined by the federal government and adjusted annually for inflation) and owns at least half of the business, an applicant can qualify for EOL assistance.

F

FDIC: Federal Deposit Insurance Company; preserves and promotes public confidence in the U.S. financial system by insuring deposits in banks and thrift institutions for at least $250,000; by identifying, monitoring and addressing risks to the deposit insurance funds; and by limiting the effect on the economy and the financial system when a bank or thrift institution fails.

FICO: Fair Isaac Corporation; yardstick used by lender to assess the amount of risk they are taking by lending money to you. It is composed of three scores, one for each of the credit bureaus: Experian, TransUnion, and Equifax.

G

Grant: Money given that is intended for a specific project or purpose; grants do not have to be repaid.

Growth: Capital appreciation; the underlying value of the investment is expected to grow. Growth investments more often than not outpace the returns on income-type investments over five to ten years or longer.

H

Hedge fund: An investment open to a limited number of investors, which allows them to bypass some regulations and invest in a wide range of activities.

HELOC: Home equity line of credit; allows you to obtain a line of credit up to a percentage of the value of your current property.

I

Income projection: A forecast of the income you expect the business to earn and the expenses you expect to accrue.

Income Statement: Shows a business's profitability.

Interest: The fee paid to borrow assets.

L

LOI: Letter of intent; document outlining an agreement between two or more parties before the agreement is finalized.

M

MCA: Mutual confidentiality agreement; a legal contract between at least two parties that outlines confidential information to restrict access to by third parties.

Microloan Program: Short-term loan offered by the SBA for start-up small businesses.

N

NCUA: National Credit Union Association; a federal agency responsible for chartering and supervising all the federal credit unions.

P

Partnership Agreement: Specify the different partners' roles in a partnership.

Piggybacking: When one company helps another company to reach its goals.

Pricing Strategy: Will help guide you in choosing the right prices for your product, based on your marketing research.

R

RFP: Request for proposal; invitation for suppliers, often through a bidding process, to submit a proposal on a specific commodity or service.

ROI: Return on investment; what you expect to get out of something in an investment.

S

SBA: Small Business Administration; independent agency of the federal government to aid, counsel, assist, and protect the interests of small business concerns.

SEC: Securities and Exchange Commission; U.S. federal agency that regulates stock and options exchanges.

Security: A document representing participation in an investment.

T

Turnkey Business: A business where someone purchases the rights to use ideas, methods, and name recognition.

V

Venture Capitalist: A professional investor who invests heavily in businesses.

W

Wholesaling: Assigning a contract to another investor for a fee.

Bibliography

Web

National Federation of Independent Business (NFIB) (**www. nfib.com**)

U.S. Small Business Administration (**www.sba.gov**)

Huntington & Williams, Privacy and Security Law Issues in Offshore Outsourcing Transactions (**www.outsourcing.com**)

Whittemore School of Business and Economics, University of New Hampshire (**http://wsbe2.unh.edu**)

Books

W.D. Bygrave, *The Portable MBA in Entrepreneurship* (John Wiley & Sons, 1994)

E.J. McCarthy, W.D. Perreault, *Basic Marketing: A Managerial Approach* (Irwin, 1990)

Robert A. Cooke, *Buy Your Own Business With Other People's Money* (John Wiley & Sons, 2005)

Michael A. Lechter, *OPM Other People's Money: How to attract Other People's Money for your investments — the ultimate leverage* (Warner Business Books, 2005)

Harold R. Lacy, *Financing Your Business Dreams with Other People's Money* (Sage Creek Press, 1998)

Robert Shemin, *How Come That Idiot's Rich And I'm Not* (Crown Publishers, 2008)

Don Debelak, *The Risk-Free Entrepreneur* (Adams Media, 2006)

Steve Hochman, *How To Sell Your Real Estate When Real Estate is Not Selling* (Friendly Note Buyers, Inc., 2007)

Author Biography

Desiree Smith-Daughety is a freelance writer, editor, and entrepreneur with a background in business sales and marketing. She writes marketing and corporate communication materials for entrepreneurs and other business entities. Visit her Web site **www.descopysmith.com** or contact her directly: des@descopysmith.com.

Index

Corporation, 276-277, 51, 86, 104, 119, 124-127, 161, 184-185, 15

Cosigning, 65

Credit score, 51, 55, 223, 256

Credit union, 278, 68, 70

D

Debt financing, 171

Diminishing returns, 209

Diversification, 276, 262

E

Executive summary, 144, 159, 254

F

Federal Deposit Insurance Company (FDIC), 61

Financial portfolio, 44, 51, 251

G

General partnership, 123, 144

Grant, 277, 95-98, 104

H

Hedge fund, 277, 260-262, 264

Home Equity Line of Credit (HELOC), 44, 251

I

Income projection, 277, 80, 155

Income statement, 278, 152, 162

Index fund, 262-263, 265

J

Joint venture, 84, 86-88

L

Lease financing, 173-174

Letter of Intent, 278, 192

Printed in Great Britain
by Amazon